The Right Place at the Wrong Time

The Right Place at the Wrong Time

THE AUTOBIOGRAPHY OF

Corné Krige

WITH PETER BILLS

Published by Zebra Press
an imprint of Struik Publishers
(a division of New Holland Publishing (South Africa) (Pty) Ltd)
PO Box 1144, Cape Town, 8000
New Holland Publishing is a member of Johnnic Communications Ltd

www.zebrapress.co.za

First published 2005

3 5 7 9 10 8 6 4

PUBLISHING MANAGER: Marlene Fryer
MANAGING EDITOR: Robert Plummer
EDITOR: Ronel Richter-Herbert
COVER AND TEXT DESIGNER: Natascha Adendorff
TYPESETTER: Monique van den Berg
INDEXER: Robert Plummer
PHOTO RESEARCHER: Colette Stott
PRODUCTION MANAGER: Valerie Kömmer

Set in 11.5 pt on 15 pt Adobe Garamond

Reproduction by Hirt & Carter (Cape) (Pty) Ltd
Printed and bound by Paarl Print, Oosterland Street, Paarl, South Africa

ISBN 1 77007 097 4

To my wife Justine, for standing by me through the tough times, and my daughter Sophia, whose arrival gave me a new perspective on life and helped me to retire at the right time

Contents

Foreword

The concept of the 'man-of-the-match' award certainly has great marketing value, and always evokes great debate among rugby supporters. However, in my opinion, it deviates slightly from the true ethos of the game of rugby. Rugby is a great game that has stood the test of time precisely because it caters for all shapes and sizes. In this ultimate team game, no man is more valuable than the next. More often than not, in fiercely contested matches, the winning team is victorious only because its communal will to succeed and the players' commitment to support each other in moments of danger are greater than that of their opponents.

Perhaps a more significant post-match award, in keeping with the spirit of rugby, would be to the player selected by his team-mates as 'the man I most want by my side in battle'.

In that case, I am sure that Corné Krige would have won most of these awards in the many matches he played for his school, his club, his province and his country. Corné gave real meaning to the concept of 'leading from the front', as his physical commitment was at times frightening to behold. Has anybody ever shed as much blood as he on the rugby field?

This book will take you on a journey, following one man's commitment to his sport. From a farm in Zambia to Paarl Boys High, where Corné was a boarder at a very young age, to his Craven Week year (where I first noticed his exceptional rugby talent), to his career at Western Province and the Stormers, to his captaincy of the Springboks and, finally, to Northampton – and everything in between! Mostly we rejoice in the story of a focused, committed athlete and leader reaching the top of his game – but we also cannot sidestep the unusual challenges, deep disappointments and turmoil he faced as a leader of men in this sometimes troubled period in our country's rugby history.

Corné Krige and the players of his era were the first to face the full reality of a game moving swiftly to professionalism, while the game itself was arguably unprepared for this change. It was also a time when sportsmen in our country grappled with the dynamics of a vastly altered and transforming social environment. Corné's story also unfolds in an extraordinarily fluid and oftentimes unstable administrative and coaching environment.

Corné used his God-given rugby and leadership talents to the utmost of his ability. While he was largely the architect of his own success, he was, however, left at the mercy of circumstances and events not of his making, which shook this nation to its core. As the title of the book implies, he was the right man in the right place, but in a very challenging period. He dealt with these difficult situations and his 'time at the crease' much like he's dealt with his autobiography – affably, steadfastly and, above all, honestly.

MORNÉ DU PLESSIS

Acknowledgements

Writing this book has been an extremely difficult thing to do, and without certain people it would never have happened. I would like to thank my mom and dad for providing my brothers and me with a loving family and sacrificing so much to give us a good education. To my brothers Pierre and Bennie, thank you for being my biggest and most loyal supporters. Then to every single coach, teacher and parent who helped shape me as a person, a big thank you. Also to Peter Bills for helping me to write this book the way I wanted it, and to the team at Zebra Press for their enthusiasm and professionalism. And lastly, a special thank you to my editor, Ronel Richter-Herbert, for all her hard work, encouragement and understanding.

Preface

I was prepared to write myself off totally to help the Springboks win test matches. I would do anything to battle the opposition, to give us the edge. Concern for my physical well-being? Absolutely none. Concern about losing friendships because I might push my teammates too hard at times? Often, the players I had to talk to were those whom I never became friends with anyway. My real friends I never had to admonish, because they understood what I expected of them.

There were only very few guys I ever had to reprimand for attitude problems. Sometimes a player would work hard, train his butt off to break into the Bok team, but from then on his attitude would slip. If a player wasn't disciplined, I would certainly talk to him. I wasn't scared to lose the player's friendship; I just told him to set an example and not to waste the opportunity given to him.

A lot of players had so much more natural talent than me. Some guys can do all sorts of things on a rugby field – things I could only dream about. These were the players I would be harshest with, because I wanted them to do well, to express the talent in the cause of my beloved Boks.

What I had to offer the game was an enduring passion and deep love for wearing the Springbok jersey. Wild cats would not have torn that jersey off me while I was playing for South Africa. I was far from being the most brilliant, the most gifted player in the history of the Springboks. There were many more with greater natural talent and skills, but I would challenge any man to say someone else wore that Springbok jersey with more pride than me.

What did it mean to me? I said more than once during my Springbok rugby career that I would rather die than lose a game.

And I meant every word. If I'd been told before a game there was a possibility I might die that day, I would not have played in a less committed manner.

I suppose, to a degree, that is a very selfish and stupid way of thinking, because I have come to understand there is more to life than Springbok rugby. Once you have a wife and child, your priorities change. But while I played rugby, I devoted everything in my power to the game. That was the way I was; that was how I played. I committed my life to rugby football during my career and my body to the Springbok cause. There were times when I was prepared to do anything to help the team, and times when that passion boiled over. Twickenham, November 2002, was both the best and worst example.

I would get mad at players who didn't want to match my commitment, and at times I got mad at myself when my efforts were not enough to avoid defeat. I ended that match against England crying my eyes out, owing to a combination of physical pain and mental anguish at our defeat. The physical battering I inflicted upon my body that day took two years off my career. Afterwards, I apologised for my actions, and I will again in this story of my life. But I do not apologise for the passion I showed in the Springbok cause.

When you get selected for the Springboks, you play for more than yourself. You are there for the team, and for the entire country. That emblem on the badge means everything to you. Once, during a conversation with former president Nelson Mandela, he said it was a miracle that we still had the springbok emblem on our jersey.

But the only reason the miracle happened was because Madiba had fought to retain it. He is well aware of how much that emblem means to me, because I once told him, very clearly, very carefully and very privately. The springbok emblem was part of my heart when I played for my country. He knows and understands that.

My times in South African rugby were a fluctuating mixture of success and failure, pleasure and pain, brutality and finesse. With the Boks, I touched the heights and plumbed the depths.

But one thing always soared above anything else in my life at the time: my sheer pride in wearing the Springbok jersey.

I played with my heart on my sleeve, much in the same way I have written this book. What I have to say may offend some, and for that I am sorry. But I have no regrets about saying what I do. All that matters is that South African rugby and, in particular, the Springbok team go from strength to strength in future years. This book frequently points out where our rugby went wrong in the past. It is my greatest wish that our rugby administrators will learn from those mistakes so that future Springbok teams will once again be acclaimed everywhere as the greatest side in the world.

As far as rugby goes, nothing else matters to me.

CORNÉ KRIGE
Cape Town
2005

1
The House of Pain

As I stood on the hallowed rugby ground at Dunedin, New Zealand, I felt a great sense of pride and history. This immense contest about to unfold, in which I was to be involved for the first time in my playing career, was what many considered to be the biggest clash in rugby football worldwide. New Zealand versus South Africa was a fixture that stirred the soul, not just of the supporters in the two countries who had adored the game down the centuries, but right around the world. When people talked about the mighty clashes between these two leading rugby nations, they spoke in awe of the great players, the proud protagonists who had given their all, either in the black outfits of the All Blacks, or the green and gold of the Springboks.

When I prepared for my first match for South Africa against New Zealand in 1999, they had been knocking lumps out of one another on international rugby grounds for seventy-eight years. The first ever game between them was played in Dunedin in 1921, and that day New Zealand emerged the victors, by 13 points to 5. But that inaugural three-test series was as hard fought and close as any game between the two nations would be ever after. South Africa won the second test 9-5 in Auckland, and, remarkably, the third test, the series decider, ended in a 0-0 draw.

By complete coincidence, my first taste of a fixture that so often resembled a sports battle was also to be at the Dunedin ground. Dunedin is a long, long way down towards the bottom of the world, close to Invercargill on the southern tip of the South Island and, from there, less than 3 000 miles to the South Pole. Very often, it feels as if the wind blowing across the Carisbrook rugby ground at Dunedin is from the polar ice cap, and heavy rain very often accompanies it.

In recent years, the climatic conditions, combined with the hostile, red-hot reception a visiting player receives on the field, has been such that locals have nicknamed Carisbrook the 'House of Pain'. As I lined up to face the All Blacks' renowned *haka* that day, I was unaware of how appropriate that nickname would prove in my case.

It was only my third full cap for the Springboks. After years of playing in the junior ranks, steadily building up towards the mighty Springboks, I had made my senior debut against Italy in Durban earlier that year. Astonishingly, I had also been made captain on my first test appearance, a rare occurrence. The then Springbok captain, Gary Teichmann, was injured, and when they offered the job to 'Rassie' Erasmus, our other back-row forward, he turned it down. He didn't want the extra burden, preferring instead to concentrate on his own game. They approached me next, and there was no way I was going to refuse the offer.

To represent the Springboks was a huge honour. To captain them in my first test was an awesome achievement. I am still the only player in the history of the game to have captained his country on his test debut and lead them to a 100-point victory! But that is exactly what happened. We beat Italy 101-0 after our 74-3 victory in the first test at Port Elizabeth a week earlier.

I should point out straight away, for those readers not so familiar with the strengths and weaknesses of international rugby teams, that Italy was a country in the second tier of the game. And we were brutally reminded of that fact in our next match, when we went to Cardiff and lost to a Welsh side that, at the time, was enjoying a resurgence under the New Zealand coach Graham Henry. I wasn't captain against Wales, as Gary Teichmann was once again fit to resume the captaincy. Nevertheless, the 19-29 defeat in Cardiff was a horrible crash to earth after starting my test career with a 101-point win.

The spectacle that greeted us in Dunedin took me completely

by surprise. As we drove through the city, we saw that all the shops had been decked out in black ribbons and bunting, and we noticed that, as the week went on, almost everyone was dressed in black. It constantly reminded us that the All Blacks were in town, and it all added up to a pretty intimidating sight. It made me sit up very quickly and realise just how intensely involved the New Zealanders were in their rugby.

Perhaps until that day, I'd been under the impression that it was only in South Africa that you could find such a fanatical following for a national rugby team. Although I knew that New Zealanders loved their rugby with a passion, I never imagined it would be as big as this!

But there is a huge difference between intense support for the home side and intimidation of the opposition. I have to stress that at no stage did I feel the latter.

Particularly in my younger days, I didn't really understand pressure or what it meant. I was so excited to go out and play for South Africa that, frankly, the worst thing for me was the inevitable waiting during the week preceding a test match. I wanted it to start right away. Mind you, the night before the New Zealand test, I began to feel pretty nervous and struggled to fall asleep. I was sharing a room with Robbie Fleck – two players, I'm sure you'll agree, who would not take a backward step against any opponent on the rugby field.

But both that night and on match day, I felt the nerves niggling away in the pit of my stomach. After all, it was only my third cap, so I was hardly a super-experienced sportsman who had seen and done it all before. In terms of understanding what it meant to confront the New Zealand All Blacks, particularly in their own backyard, this was my first time. And, as I was to find out during the course of my career, there was always something more intense – perhaps even more sinister– about having to face the All Blacks in Dunedin.

But wherever you play a major rugby match, especially an

international, you have got to try to stay as calm and relaxed as possible beforehand. It is essential that players learn to control the adrenalin they will feel surging through their veins. If you start getting too bouncy and run around the hotel, you will be knackered by the time the kick-off arrives. You must try to control that adrenalin, hard as it is at times. I used to think that a massive adrenalin rush would give me an edge on the rugby field, but later in my career I found that it never flowed as intensely as it used to in me. But, even so, I was still not concerned for my personal health and well-being when I played in a match. In fact, later on I would be extremely calm before matches. I learnt to control the adrenalin.

Every All Black match is preceded by a rendition of the *haka*, the traditional tribal challenge that the Maoris used to lay down before all visitors to their land. For the tourist, it may be an exciting, fun experience to see it performed. But, believe me, when you are a Springbok rugby player and it is performed just a few yards away from where you are standing, and up to 40 000 people are roaring their support, there can be no room for doubt that this war dance is for real.

On that day, the power of the occasion suddenly hit me, and I was very emotional as they performed the *haka*. This moment was the realisation of a twelve-year-old dream, ever since I had first picked up a rugby ball and played with meaning. Here I was: I'd climbed the mountain; now the view from the summit was heady indeed.

When you start playing rugby as a youngster, you hardly dare dream that one day you might represent your country. But, as that dream eventually comes within reach, you begin to experience a deep desire to see it fulfilled. Taking that final step to achieving the honour becomes almost an obsession, a ravenous hunger, if you like, that can only be satisfied by your selection to the team, and then playing in the game itself. I thought, too, of all the hard work, the mental and physical pain I had gone through to get to where I was, and the many setbacks I had endured and overcome along the way.

All of these things flitted through my mind as I stood on the field, proudly wearing my Springbok jersey, ready to take my place in the long line of young men who had been combatants in this massive rugby tradition spanning almost a century. Those thoughts, those emotional feelings, combined to make the tears well up in my eyes while the All Blacks performed the *haka*, and I could feel them trickling down my face. A grown man crying? Sure, and I was not about to apologise for it. It is very exciting when you generate that much emotion. I let the tears flow. I knew that, soon enough, my blood would follow the tears, for I was ready to lay my body on the line. I understood implicitly what was required of me: courage, mental and physical bravery, utter commitment, and a disregard for the safety of my body for the eighty minutes that would follow.

When you become locked into a mindset that enables you to have no fear of any impending pain you may experience, it is almost as if you become a different person, a different animal. That was certainly true of me when I played at the top level. Sometimes that transformation was for the better; on occasions, it was for the worse, because, to be frank, at times I could not control that animal. When it was kept in check, it was very effective. It meant that I showed huge commitment and was prepared to do almost anything, go through just about any pain imaginable, for the team and victory. Alas – and I am the first to admit this – when the animal was out of control, it could be a liability.

Of course, various people react differently to certain situations. We don't all have the same mentality. We see and experience things differently; not everyone expresses himself in exactly the same way. For me, in the early part of my career especially, I put very high expectations on myself, but not to the point where I would lose control of the beast.

But later on, I felt a serious responsibility to the teams I represented: chiefly, the Stormers and the Springboks. And I found that it was then, when I had a huge stake in the team I was playing for, that I started getting involved in the odd incident, because I was taking my rugby far too seriously. By then, it wasn't just a game any more. For example, I was familiar with the finances of the Western Province Rugby Union, and that intensified the pressure. If we lost two or three games on the trot, I knew that the spectator-numbers at Newlands could decline from around 40 000 to 30 000, and I was fully aware of the Union's budget. A defeat could therefore have serious financial consequences, which put a huge strain on certain people in the Union.

But, talking about pressure, our coach in that 1999 Tri-Nations series was clearly under the cosh. And his frailties had begun to show. Less than ten months earlier, Nick Mallett had been hugely fêted as the South African coach who had inspired the Boks to a record-equalling seventeen-match winning run, spanning the months from August 1997 to November 1998. In that time, Mallett's teams had developed a formidable reputation by beating Australia and Ireland three times each, New Zealand, England, France, Wales and Scotland twice each, and Italy once. Memories of the Springboks' test series defeat to the British Lions earlier in 1997, under Carel du Plessis, had perhaps not been completely forgotten (no Springbok fan *ever* completely forgets the defeats), but they had certainly been pushed into the background by this extraordinary run of form.

Alas, since that golden run, things had become more difficult. England broke the spell, winning 13-7 in a hard contest at Twickenham in our last game of 1998, and, although we'd started 1999 with those two thumping wins over Italy, the defeat in Wales that followed was a significant setback. No one was under any illusions on that score.

But it wasn't just the defeat against Wales that made me think Mallett was buckling under the pressure. He had selected Gaffie du Toit at outside half for the test in Dunedin, but the day before, after the captain's run, which is really the final, light run-out before the actual match, he had made it clear that he was very concerned about Gaffie's defence. So he asked three or four of the guys to run against Gaffie, in simulated attacking movements by the 'opposition'. He wanted Gaffie to make the decision about which of the runners he should take.

I was standing behind him, and, in five runs, Gaffie selected the wrong guy four times. No matter what we read into that, I felt Nick was wrong in making him do it, because I was sure it would break his confidence. South Africa was looking for a new, young No. 10 now that older players such as Henry Honiball had moved on, and I really couldn't see how this extra training-ground test, thrust on Gaffie so late in the week, could help. As it transpired, Gaffie had a really bad game the next day. I believed ever after that the late training session was one of the reasons. Nick sowed seeds of doubt in Gaffie's mind, but that was because of the pressure on Nick, resulting from our loss to Wales.

But as the two sides lined up for the kick-off at Dunedin that day, my mind was focused on only one thing: how could I produce my best in the match and help my team to win? Up to that point in my career, Carisbrook, Dunedin was certainly the most hostile environment I had ever been in as a rugby player, but I knew I had to focus intensely on the task that lay ahead.

I have two main memories of that match. The worst memory I will come to soon, but the other concerned the sheer pace of the game from the kick-off. It was something I had never experienced before in my life. The intensity was huge, but the speed at which the play went on was almost frightening. In the first ten minutes, Josh Kronfeld, the New Zealand breakaway forward who was my direct opponent, always seemed to be a couple of yards ahead of me in all I did and wherever I went.

Kronfeld was a very good back-row forward, in the finest tradition of New Zealand flankers. And they've had plenty of 'greats' in that position in their time: men such as Andy Leslie, Graham Mourie, Kronfeld himself, and now Richie McCaw, whom I rate as one of the best ever. Whatever I did, I found myself just behind Kronfeld, which was not only infuriating, but also very revealing in what it told me about the standards I would have to match if I wanted to enjoy a lengthy stay in the Springbok side.

That isn't to say I didn't make any tackles, didn't begin to do the job for which I had been selected, which was a combination of winning the loose ball on the ground, being a link man in movements involving the backs, and helping my fellow forwards with the physical requirements of a test match. If you combine all those tasks and do them well in a match with as much pressure as an international, then, believe me, there really shouldn't be much left in the tank by the time you come off the field at the end. As someone once said, never end a match with even a quarter of your energy levels still left. You should have given absolutely everything for your team.

I certainly meant to do that against New Zealand in Dunedin. So much so that, even now, when I look back years later, I am still deeply frustrated and haunted by the memory of what had happened next. The game had been going on for about ten minutes when the New Zealand fullback Christian Cullen, a genius with the ball in hand going forward, broke through our defensive line. I went to tackle him, but didn't notice our burly prop forward, Os du Randt, also lining him up in his sights. Basically, Du Randt, who has been one of *the* great servants of Springbok rugby, tackled Cullen hard, but straight into my leg. My foot was already planted, ready to make the tackle, and all my weight was on it. The impact dislocated my left knee: I suffered, in medical terminology, an anterior cruciate rupture and a bicep femoris rupture. The blow wrecked the bicep femoris, ripping it off the bone. Such damage, I was told later, usually detaches the whole nerve, and if that had happened, I would have had a drop foot (when the nerve doesn't work and the whole foot drops) for the rest of my life. I certainly wouldn't have played rugby ever again.

The television footage shows the exact moment when my knee virtually disintegrated. Not surprisingly, the moment it happened, I knew I was in serious trouble. I lay on the ground, trying not to move, because whenever I did, indescribable pain would shoot through my whole body. It was absolute agony.

Our physio, Wayne Diesel, rushed on and said, 'What's wrong?'

I replied, 'I've hurt my knee very badly.'

He took hold of the knee, and could swing it nearly 180 degrees. Immediately, he spoke through his microphone to our assistant coach in the stand, Alan Solomons, and said, 'Corné is off.' Apparently Solly replied, 'Can he try and stay on for another ten minutes?' All I heard was Diesel saying, 'Solly, you don't understand. He's f***ed.'

I was loaded onto a stretcher, and then they nearly dropped me while carrying me off. I was in huge agony. I had never been physically ill through pain, but felt as close to it then as I imagined you ever could be. I was given pain-killing injections at the ground, and the All Black doctor saw me. He was a very nice guy and helped me as much as he could.

Looking back, my overriding memory of that incident and the aftermath is firstly of the pain, but also of the loneliness that followed. By the end of the test match, something other than my injury was a major talking point among the Springboks. We had lost 0-28 at the House of Pain, and had to play Australia the very next week. People were sad for me, but the result was a bigger issue.

My match had ended prematurely, my Tri-Nations campaign was over and my whole season was finished. But little did I know what lay ahead of me in terms of mental trauma. I had to endure a long, lonely trip back to South Africa. The medical people in New Zealand gave me injections in my stomach because they were concerned about the danger of a blood clot forming on the flight home. Of course, with so serious an injury, you shouldn't really fly until it has healed somewhat, but I wanted to get home as soon as possible. When you are ill or injured, you need familiar surroundings in which to be treated and recuperate.

Except that I was a long, long way from home. The knee was heavily strapped up, to try to get me through the ordeal, and with the aid of crutches, I was helped onto an Air New Zealand flight across the Tasman Sea to Australia. There, I boarded a Qantas flight after immediately being upgraded to first class, something you would normally make the absolute most of. But in my condition, I was just grateful for the extra legroom, and began the long journey back to South Africa – a seemingly endless flight from Sydney to Johannesburg, via Perth in Western Australia. I have to say that, despite the kindness of the Qantas staff on board the aeroplane, it was an absolutely horrible trip, as I was in such pain.

I had telephoned Bruce McLaughlin, my physio at Western Province, from New Zealand, and told him I would come straight to see him. The pain was increasing, as the pain-killing injections were wearing off. I needed to have the knee looked at straight away. It also played on my mind that the Rugby World Cup was due to take place later that year, and, although I knew I had a serious injury, I still hoped against hope, as all sportsmen are inclined to do, that I might somehow be given a promising diagnosis regarding my chances of recovering in time. There were three months to go, and I longed for encouraging news.

At first, there seemed to be some hope. After taking off all the bandages, Bruce listened as I told him what had happened, but initially he didn't think that the anterior cruciate had gone. Just before seeing me, Bruce had been treating a woman who had suffered a leg injury. When I limped into the cubicle and sat on the bed, Bruce inadvertently didn't quite close the curtain. When the bandages came off, my knee was so loose that it almost seemed to be hanging. Bruce lifted the leg, moved it a little, said nothing and walked away to fetch something. While he was gone, this woman, who clearly knew who I was, poked her head around the curtain and, quite unprompted, said, 'Oh dear, that must surely mean the end of your career. You won't play again.'

After forty hours of travelling, excruciating pain, and constant worry and fear about what I might be told, I needed this advice like a hole in the head. I ignored the woman and she eventually left, but afterwards my anger really built up. So much so that I asked Bruce for her phone number. I wanted to ring her up and give her a piece of my mind. But Bruce just said, 'Forget it.' And of course, he was right.

Bruce phoned a surgeon who was based in Cape Town and whom I already knew rather too well, 'Spike' Erasmus. The injury was sufficiently serious for Spike to come back from his holiday early, and I met him at the Panorama Medi-Clinic on the outskirts of Cape Town. His diagnosis was that the cruciate ligament was probably gone, but he couldn't be sure until he opened me up on the operating table. He did that very soon, within a day or so. Yet, as I lay in hospital prior to the operation, I was still desperately hoping that they'd find it wasn't too bad after all, and they could get me fit again in time for the World Cup in Wales.

When I awoke from the operation late the next day and began to emerge through the fog of anaesthetic, Spike sat down on the bed and explained the situation. He didn't pull any punches. 'Your cruciate was totally ruptured,' he said. 'You have no hope whatever of playing in the World Cup, and you'll be out of rugby for at least six to eight months.' I lay there and took this shattering news much like a boxer trapped on the ropes absorbs a series of body blows. The only respite from such a mental hammering was that Spike felt he had repaired the damage well.

'Although of course we cannot tell at this stage, you have a chance of making a full recovery,' he assured me. I stayed in hospital for two or three days, and was on crutches for six weeks. Three days after returning home from hospital, I started my first session of rehab, in the swimming pool. You feel horrible after any operation, but I was determined to attack the gargantuan task I knew lay before me. I worked constantly with Bruce, and when he suggested we attempt a short session in the swimming pool, just to try to get some movement in my leg, I agreed. It was agony, of course. So much so that, when I came out of the pool and headed back to his practice, the combination of the recent anaesthetic and the pool session proved too much for me. My system was so wrecked that I fainted.

That was the start of eight months of tortuous hard work and pain. Basically, you have no choice but to work through the pain barrier. Believe me, the pain barrier is not a myth in people's minds or writers' imaginations – it really exists. With an injury like mine, you have to break down the scar tissue, but initially you have to keep the leg still for a long time to allow the ligaments to heal. In fact, I did not attempt my first jog for five months.

I didn't tell anyone at the time, but I must confess that I had serious concerns – not about whether I would ever play again, but whether I'd recover sufficiently to make it back to the top level. It takes a great deal of hard work to recover from a bad cruciate injury, and, of course, you lose so much speed over the course of all those months. I worried, too, that if I ever suffered another bad cruciate injury, I'd not be tough enough mentally to go through the whole painful process again. I feared that that would be the end of me.

And it is not just about the pain levels. When you are a top-class sportsman, you train hard every week, enduring physical discomfort and pain, as well as mental torment, much of the time. That is all right when a fit player gets his reward at the end of every week. He plays in a match. But when you have a bad injury, it gets to you that you're not playing. The recovery process is frighteningly monotonous, and there is no reward for at least six to seven months. Work, work, work, but no play: anyone can be driven mad by such a regime. There are plenty of times when you feel really sorry for yourself.

However, I was very glad not to have to worry about one issue. Both the Stormers, the Super 12 franchise based in Cape Town, and the Springboks, with which I had contracts, were most supportive, and assured me that I need not worry about my contract being terminated with either of them. Under most such sports contracts, the employer has the option to terminate your contract if you fail to recover from an injury after six months.

But neither organisation put pressure on me to return before I was properly ready, and I was very grateful for that. When you have suffered so serious an injury, it is important in every sense to remain positive. The last thing you want to be worrying about is whether your job will still be there for you if you don't recover within a certain period.

Of course, the 1999 World Cup had long since come and gone by the time I was taking my first tentative steps towards regaining complete fitness. I watched the tournament with a combination of fascination and longing, aware that I'd been too young to participate in the 1995 event, which South Africa had hosted and so memorably won four years earlier. Now, 1999 had come and gone, and I'd missed that too.

I began to wonder whether I was fated never to appear in a Rugby World Cup, a thought that depressed me no end. But long before I'd know that, I faced a critical test in my recovery. Would I ever be able to play again at the level I had known? Or was my international career destined to end after only ten minutes into my third appearance for South Africa? Little did I know that this would be the story of my rugby life, the highs and lows coming in rapid succession throughout my career.

2
Bush Baby

I was born in Lusaka, Zambia, on 21 March 1975, the third boy of Corrie and Cecilia Krige. There was general celebration all over Zambia that year … not in honour of my birth, but at the opening of the long-awaited Tanzania–Zambia railway. It stretched from the Zambian copper belt, 322 miles north of Lusaka, to Dar es Salaam, the great Tanzanian port on the Indian Ocean. Happiness was widespread, as the opening of the line reduced the country's dependency on the rail route via Rhodesia for its exports. But within five years, white rule in Rhodesia would be swept away in any case, and Zimbabwe would emerge, under Robert Mugabe.

In the 1880s, Northern Rhodesia, as this part of Africa was then known, came under the administration of the British South Africa Company of Cecil John Rhodes. Later, in 1924, it became a British protectorate, but it was not for another forty years that independence was finally achieved, when Kenneth Kaunda became president of Zambia.

Pierre, my eldest brother, was six years old when I was born. Bennie was three. My grandfather, Dad's father Pieter Daniël, had moved from the old Orange Free State to Fort Jameson to start a farm there in 1947, although my father had been born in South Africa, in a place called Klerksdorp. My grandmother, mother's mom, whose name was Cecilia Lindeque, although everyone knew her as Babsie, had been born in Lusaka.

George Gregan, later to become captain of the Australian rugby team, was also born in Lusaka, two years before me. That must be some achievement for a city in the middle of Africa, to have produced two baby boys who would both later become the captains of their respective countries' rugby teams.

Mom and Dad lived on a 3 000-hectare farm, approximately forty-five kilometres outside the Zambian capital. They grew maize and a bit of tobacco, and raised a few hundred head of cattle. There was a huge lake on the land, so big that I remember people used to come and water-ski on it with their boats. As kids, we would play around in the water, a welcome relief from the daytime temperatures, which would often exceed 40°C (106°F). Although it cooled down at night, even in wintertime it was still hot up there by day. I remember the oppressive heat, the dust and the flies, but also the beauty and grandeur of the countryside. The great skies seemed to tower over us, stretching all the way, we imagined, up to heaven.

Mom and Dad gave us a Christian upbringing. Dad worked on the farm and was always busy. As any farmer will tell you, there is always something to do. Mother taught in the farm school, yet she and Dad still managed to spend quality time with us, especially at weekends. As soon as I was old enough, I used to join my brothers in their activities around the farm. We'd go shooting at birds with airguns, ride bikes, and play with some of the other kids who lived either on the farm or nearby. We had television, but only the ZNBC (Zambian National Broadcasting Company), which showed boring programmes that certainly didn't interest us kids. Apart from watching the news, we would spend our free time outside, engaged in various activities.

Sometimes we would spend time with Sampson, our chef and cleaner, who worked for my parents. In fact, he still works for my mother, and has now been with our family for more than forty years. Sampson would help us build things, tell us where to go if we wanted something in particular, and generally be a fount of wisdom and advice. He also taught us the Nyanja language spoken by the local people. We all learnt a lot from him.

In Zambia, it would usually get dark at about six in the evening, and we would see the most magnificent sunsets, the sky painted in incredibly vibrant colours, many of them with a fiery glow. I remember those sunsets to this day – they were simply spectacular.

Once nature's show had ended and darkness fell, we would eat around the table together at about 7 p.m. Then, perhaps after a game of darts, we'd start getting ready for bed. In those days, I hated reading, and never read for pleasure or recreation. Today, I am glad to say, I do enjoy it.

People who live on farms are early risers, and we'd be up and about by 6.30 most mornings, as the sun was coming up. We therefore tended to go to bed at a reasonable hour to get the sleep we all needed for another day in the open air.

My favourite time of the year was in June, when we would set off for our annual hunting trip to the bush. We'd load up the pickups and drive for many hours over rough terrain through the scrubby bush, where all you could see were stark trees that had wilted under the power of the sun, the baked, cracked ground, and the lizards that darted here and there.

We would eventually decide on a site beside the river in the Luangwa Valley, unload all our gear and start to make camp. A fire would be lit, the food cooked by Sampson, water would be boiled, and we'd sit out as the daylight began to fade and night came, with the silence broken only by the occasional cry of a bird or the sound of an animal some way off. The fire would both warm us during the chilly night and protect us against predators. We would sleep on the mattresses we had brought with us; we had no tents.

Fishing was also one of our activities, and we'd try to land the tiger fish that were in the Luangwa. But they're very aggressive fish and could give you a huge bite if you got your fingers anywhere near their mouths. In fact, they'd probably take off part of your finger. The other fish we caught was bream, and there was plenty of it in the river.

I loved those trips. It was awesome country, so wild and untouched by the hand of mankind. That was what appealed to me most. I still go back to those parts on hunting and camping trips, and always will. The countryside reminds me of my childhood and the beauty of Africa. The people there are wonderful too.

I shot my first buffalo up there as a grown-up, something I had wanted to do since I was a boy. The buffalo is one of the so-called Big Five, which include the elephant, lion, leopard and rhino. The buffalo is a dangerous animal, and sometimes the herds are anything between 300 and 2 000 strong. I'd shot game like impala, warthogs and kudu from the age of nine, but never a buffalo.

I've never shot a lion, nor do I ever want to, as there are not enough of them. The same applies to the other animals in the Big Five. But buffalo are there in great numbers.

Up there, maybe 700 kilometres into the bush and not far from the Malawi border, you are as close to nature as it's possible to be. There is no radio or television or anything much: just the animals and the absolute beauty of the country. That is enough for me; I don't need any other pleasures. As a child, we'd go in a group and take trackers and skinners with us. The Luangwa Valley, where we went, was one of the best areas to see animals. Every July, we would buy a licence to hunt twelve animals during the two weeks we were there. We'd have a braai every night and cook some of the meat. Although we would take fresh vegetables and potatoes with us, everything else we ate was whatever we could shoot or catch in the river. We boiled water from the river on the fire and used it for drinking.

Our whole family would go on those trips: Mom and Dad and my two brothers, and we would be joined by my Uncle Ouboet and Aunt Bennie, and their two daughters Magda and Cecilia, who were the same ages as my two older brothers. It was one of two times in the year that we would be sure to get together with them. We'd have great fires that lasted most of the night, and, when you lay down to sleep, you could hear hippos, hyenas and other animals. It was like living two different lives: one in the city during school time, and then one in the bush during the holidays. No prizes for guessing which I preferred.

Now, this is just what South Africans should do more of – go camping in the bush. I am convinced that if you enjoy nature and wild animals, you are less likely to pollute the world in general, and your own body in particular.

The other time we got together with our family was at Christmas. Then there would be a major feast, even though one would be dripping with perspiration from the heat. Sampson would cook lots of different types of meat: a leg of lamb, perhaps a large joint of pork, plenty of steaks, plus a chicken or two. I loved eating any kind of meat, but in those days trying to get me to eat my vegetables was like trying to wriggle free from Dad's grasp when you were getting a hiding: it just couldn't be done! Today I understand the health advantages of good, fresh vegetables, and I eat them regularly.

Other things I always remember about growing up in that part of Africa are the great storms and the very high rainfall. Often, the heat of the day would have been oppressive, and, somehow, one seemed to sense when it was just *too* hot. Then a massive storm would come that night. It would begin far off, a low yet discernible grumbling noise that always frightened me when I was little. It was like retribution when you had been naughty: you knew what was coming and there wasn't a thing you could do about it.

The storms would often start in the late afternoon or at night-time. Gradually, the sky would blacken and the rumbling would become clearer as the storm drew closer. Great forks of lightning would flash across the sky, and then the rumbling would turn into crashes of thunder as the storm came overhead. Usually, by that time, I'd long since left my bed, scared to death, and crept in with Mom and Dad in the next room! But at last the crashing would diminish in intensity and the storm would go rumbling on its way, still heard a long way off but no longer a threat. By that time, of course, the deluge had descended, the rain hammering on the tin roof of our old farmhouse. The next morning, there would be that special, unmistakeable smell of rain on the dust, and we kids would go playing in the big puddles that had formed by the side of the road.

The harsh environment definitely influenced my upbringing. With two older brothers in the family, I quickly learnt that, generally speaking, you had to fight for what you wanted, and be pretty damn good at it, too. If you were a wimp and easily pushed around, you never ended up with much. So we used to fight like hell. If Dad wasn't around when a fight broke out, Mom would tell us to get out of the house and sort it out on the lawn. It always ended in tears, and not just mine.

Sweets were a particular source of trouble. We didn't get a lot of them living out on a farm. Although Dad went in to Lusaka perhaps once a week on business, I didn't go with him and he certainly didn't go to buy us sweets. Also, the local sweets were not so tasty, and South African products were not imported at the time. It was therefore a real treat when people came to visit and brought a bag of 'foreign' sweets for us boys, and there was usually only one way that shares were decided: by fighting. There would always be big fights, sometimes followed by a good hiding from Dad when things got out of hand.

If we youngsters stepped out of line, Dad would belt us. Although it hurt at the time, you tended to learn from your mistakes and tried to avoid more of the same in the future. I'm sure that was the intended effect. But this kind of discipline helped to toughen you up.

I had hidings from my father on various occasions, but, unlike some people nowadays, I don't believe they did me any harm. I don't have a problem with corporal punishment, and, should I ever have a son, I would give him a hiding if he were naughty enough. I don't think a smack on the bum is a bad thing and, in fact, I shudder to think what I would be like now if I hadn't been given hidings in my early years. It reminded you that there were limits, and if you crossed the line, you were in for it.

We had two homes up on the farm: one where the school was, and one that Dad had built on a rise next to a massive anthill. This house had beautiful views down to the lake. There was also a huge garden, probably the size of a rugby field. It was a really nice farmhouse, with four bedrooms, and in the springtime the flowers that my mother had planted in the garden looked beautiful.

There were some wild animals, such as kudu and reedbuck, to be found within a reasonable distance of the farm. The kudus' long legs carried their bodies with great balance and grace. Quite often, usually after bush fires, one of the farm workers would find a baby animal, maybe a small antelope, whose parents had died in the fire. They would bring it back to the farm and we would rear it with a bottle of milk until it had grown sufficiently and was strong enough to survive on its own in the wild. When we released them, invariably they would still hang around the area, and you wondered whether they would readapt to their normal habitat. But then one morning you would wake up and they'd be gone. You'd never see them again. In one sense you felt sad, but also pleased that nature had taken its course.

Sometimes there were as many as seventy kids at Bardy Farm School. They would be a mixture of children from surrounding farms who would board at the farm during the week and then go home at weekends. Having so many children around made it a lively place during the week. I started at the school in 1979, when I was just four. You'd have your special friends, of course, but with so many children around, there was always someone to have a game with, to get up to some kind of mischief with. There weren't any built-in prejudices about black or white: you had friends of both races and you tended to accept them as they were. In those days, youngsters growing up further south in South Africa were not able to say the same. Then again, we had plenty of servants on the farm, which meant we led a pretty spoilt lifestyle. We certainly didn't have to do many chores.

As we got older, we were able to go exploring further from the farm on bikes. By then, Pierre was on a motorbike and enjoying the experience – much to the envy of his younger brothers.

But one game we never played was rugby. I don't think I'd even seen a rugby ball at the time, and I certainly had no interest in the sport. We never had a rugby ball, and not because my parents didn't want to buy us one – we just weren't interested in the game. There were a few rugby clubs in Zambia, mainly ex-pat, but the game was not regarded as anything other than a very minor sport up there. And to be honest, sports were way down on my list of activities as a youngster on the farm. I was too keen on the outdoor life, doing all the things I've mentioned, to be bothered about most sports, including rugby. I might have heard of it, but I simply wasn't interested. Yet, deep in the archives of South African rugby, you will find a distant relation of mine who had been a fine rugby player. Japie Krige was very distantly related to me on my father's side. Born in 1879, he played five tests for the Springboks between 1903 and 1906, and he lived to the ripe old age of eighty-two, before he died in 1961.

I spent the first seven years of my life in these idyllic surroundings. I just loved the country and being in it all the time. The first time I ever went into Lusaka with Dad, I remember thinking what a horrible, dirty place a city was. I couldn't wait to get back to the farm and the countryside later that day, quite content if I never saw a city again. There seemed to be simplicity to life on the farm, a sense of unity and closeness with others that I enjoyed. You made your own entertainment, shared the company of your brothers and your friends, and found plenty to do just by being out in the wild. I hadn't the slightest urge to head for the city, and I assumed that nothing would alter this perfect lifestyle for many years.

How wrong I was. At the farm school, we had really only

covered the basic rudiments of an early education: English, some elementary maths and a little geography. The curriculum wasn't very sophisticated, as one would expect from a farm school. There was a wide variety of youngsters with, inevitably, varying learning capabilities.

None of this troubled me, of course. I was always happiest when running off after school finished in the afternoons, throwing down my books in my room and racing outside to play with one of my friends. It never occurred to me that I might one day have to give up this life, all that I had known thus far, and travel thousands of miles to another country and a strange school in order to get a better education. But one day, when I was still only six years old, my parents called me into our living room, sat me down and told me that was exactly what was going to happen.

In the year I turned seven, I would board an aircraft at Lusaka airport and fly all the way to South Africa, to attend a school in Paarl, in the Western Cape. I think the idea was sold to me by focusing on what would be a hugely exciting event: my first ever aeroplane journey. Certainly, I was so excited at the thought that I overlooked the harder realities of the situation – namely, that I would be leaving my parents behind in Zambia to head off to a strange country I'd never seen before, to attend a school where I would know no one.

When the day came to leave, I remember being a very happy camper. I suppose that was to be expected: the excitement of boarding the aircraft and flying for the first time in my life. But when we arrived at Lusaka airport and I saw how moved my parents were by my leaving, I started to rethink the whole situation. It was an emotional moment, and even to this day I still hate saying goodbye because of all the goodbyes we said during my childhood. It didn't take me long to realise that I wasn't going to see my parents for three months. Once that reality set in, it became very tough indeed.

I first saw Paarl Boys Primary School at the end of January

1982. Paarl is an attractive town, with tree-lined streets and lovely gabled homes. Its main street, which is eleven kilometres long, runs beside the Berg River. The early settlers arrived around 1690, when the town was founded, and the name Paarl originates from the Dutch word *peerlbergh*, which means 'Pearl Mountain'. An early explorer saw three smooth domes after a rain shower, the effects of the mica chips embedded in the mountain granite that glisten in the sun, making the rock look like some kind of glittery pearl.

My overriding feeling during those first few days at my new school was one of loneliness. My two brothers were in more advanced grades, and I therefore didn't see that much of them during the week. When I think about those days now, I still feel uncomfortable with the experience. But then it must have been just as tough for my parents to send us all away to school.

My parents chose Paarl for two reasons: they had friends in the town with whom I could stay during the week, and my grandparents lived in the Cape and we could visit them at weekends. That was fine on Saturdays and Sundays, but it still left a long week to get through largely on my own in a strange home. In that environment, you quickly learn to do things for yourself. You find your feet very quickly, because you have to. There is no choice: it's sink or swim. Of course, very often it's like a duck on a lake. All appears calm, serene even, on the surface, but below, the duck's legs are going a mile a minute. It was like that with me. Many a night I cried myself to sleep in those early days, burying my face in the pillow so that my parents' friends, whom I was boarding with, wouldn't hear my sobs. Outwardly you try to play the macho man, but inside you're hurting badly.

When I had problems, I went to my grandmother. Yet I was never really able to discuss that much with her, as the age gap was too great. In time, this lack of guidance would get me into trouble. I felt I had no one close to me whom I could ask for help. So I would try to sort out my problems myself. That's all right if you are older and more mature, but at seven or eight, there are decided disadvantages to such a situation. Emotionally, it was difficult for me to deal with life in general. My isolation made me a bit of a rebel, and I tended to use brute force to sort out my problems. It wasn't the best idea.

I was a little brat, an angry young man who didn't like authority. I'm still not sure why – perhaps I resented having to leave home so young. That might have had something to do with it. But I never took my anger out on the family I was staying with or my grandparents, for the simple reason that I was always too glad to see them. Nor was I angry with my parents for their decision to send me away to school. Now that I have a child of my own, I realise how difficult it must have been for them.

Financially, our education in South Africa was also a burden. Eventually we no longer flew between Lusaka and Cape Town; we had to drive.

At school, I took my hidings when I had to, and just got on with things. My father had taught me that there was a price to pay if you stepped out of line.

I remember one occasion – I was about twelve – when I poured a bottle of peroxide over my hair. I think I just wanted some attention, but it looked ridiculous and I felt a fool as soon as I'd done it. Worse still, I had to shave off my hair and let it grow back, during which time it looked even worse. The master gave me a good hiding: two strikes with the cane. But that wasn't the only time I was in his study getting caned. It happened quite often, usually for being naughty or cheeky in class, or not doing my homework. I think the most strikes I ever had were six, for drinking at the school. But that happened when I was sixteen.

The couple I stayed with, the Jouberts, were very kind and well-meaning people. They lived just outside Paarl on a farm that produced wines under the Backsberg label. Mr Joubert was the farm manager. There were also some pigs and goats on the farm, which was much smaller than the one I was used to in Zambia, and there was no real bush there. It was much closer to suburbia. The Jouberts had a son my age, François, and I suppose the family had been chosen for that reason.

I was quite small for my age, but also a bit of a bully. I had a will of my own and was extremely naughty at times. Although I wasn't into things like smoking or drinking, certainly not at that young age, I was irritable, and François and I had the odd scrap. I'm sure he sometimes felt I'd invaded his territory, which I can understand.

At times, through no fault of the Jouberts, I just didn't want to be there. The trouble was, there were no other options. My parents couldn't get the kind of education they wanted for me in Zambia, and South Africa was the nearest and the best choice.

At least in Cape Town my brothers and I could see our grandparents at weekends, which meant they virtually took on the role of alternative parents. It was nice for them, but essential for a seven-year-old away from home for the first time, given that I only saw my brothers occasionally.

When a child leaves home at such a young age to go to school, it is inevitable that his relationship with his parents will change. Although they remain your mother and father, they are no longer hands-on parents. I want to stress that this wasn't their fault. They could have been selfish and kept us at home in Zambia to attend a small school there, thus denying us a quality education. But if they'd done that, I don't think I'd ever have become a Springbok rugby player. They didn't choose that option, however; they chose what would ultimately be best for us. I am still grateful to them for their selfless decision.

But those early years, from seven to twelve, were very difficult for me. I wasn't overly keen on schoolwork and I struggled to adapt to life away from home. Even though we went back to Zambia at the end of each term, being on the farm with my parents became a pleasure tinged with pain as the time neared for us to return to Paarl and the start of a new term. I hated those last few days, knowing what was coming. When I got back to school after each holiday, it took me quite some time to adapt. Once, I got into an argument with an older boy whom I didn't like at all. Not long after, I saw him on his bike and threw a broomstick into the spokes of the wheel. The bike crashed and he came hurtling off. I knew I would be in for it if he caught me, so I took off, running as fast as I could.

Quite soon, I saw a road ahead, but was too busy looking behind me to see if I was getting away to notice a car driving towards me. I ran straight into the side of it, bashing my elbow and hurting my leg before falling over into the road. The driver stopped, but I just wanted to get away. However, the man saw me hobbling off, and followed. I made for my grandmother's apartment and managed to get there, closely followed by this guy, who turned out to be a doctor. I apologised for what had happened and he checked me over, putting stitches in my elbow.

This incident somehow typified this mostly unhappy time for me. But if I thought I'd been through tough times, I was only kidding myself. What happened next proved to be one of the most shattering moments of my whole life.

3
The School of Hard Knocks

Christmas 1986 started as a normal holiday. My brothers and I flew home from Cape Town to Lusaka, to be met by my father at the airport. But Mom wasn't there. On the drive out to the farm, we tried to find out why. But Dad wasn't talking much. We assumed when we got there she'd be around the farm, in the kitchen or somewhere. But she wasn't.

It soon became clear that something was seriously wrong. Eventually my father sat us down at the kitchen table and told us the truth. Mom wasn't there because they had split up. Dad had met another woman.

My mother had left and was staying with my uncle outside Lusaka. Christmas was about a week away. Happy Christmas everyone.

Even today, all these years later, recalling that awful time brings pain to my heart. I was eleven, Bennie fourteen and Pierre seventeen. Three strong young lads? Yes, sure, until we were confronted with that news. I vividly remember the three of us sitting down and crying our eyes out.

All we knew was that our parents, whom we dearly loved and respected, were no longer together. We were no longer a family. Suddenly, everything seemed empty and meaningless.

I railed against my dad, and told him what I thought of him. For an awful long time afterwards, I held him responsible for what had happened. I felt that the one thing that had been there for me to fall back on in my life, the only thing I knew and regarded as safe and certain, had been broken. Although I was living far away from home, I always felt that back in Zambia there was a family home and two loving parents waiting for me to return. But this news seemed to threaten all the stability I had so often looked on as a kind of salvation.

A few days later Mom visited and explained why she had not been at the airport. The atmosphere was awful, and it was a horrible Christmas. Of course, being young, I hoped they might get back together again. At the time, divorce was almost unheard of. Today, people separate far too easily, but in those days, it was very different.

In the end, Mom and Dad got divorced. And even now, I still feel the same way I did then: divorce is a lose-lose situation for everybody involved. There are no winners, and I certainly don't think parents understand what their children go through. Looking back now, I still find it one of the most painful times of my life. I can see what damage the split and then the divorce did to our family.

Although I had been a bit naughty before my parents' split, it compounded the problem. So much so that, at one stage around that time, I was in serious danger of going off the rails. It was touch and go for me. I began to keep the wrong company, with guys who were involved in drinking and smoking. It all sounds quite innocent now, but I came from a really conservative background, and what I was being sucked into was not good.

Yet, for some reason, I didn't go any further down that path. One day, as though I had suddenly woken up from a bad dream, I just decided it wasn't for me. I simply realised that I didn't like what I saw, so I drifted away from that crowd. I had been a horrible kid, but in the end perhaps you have to figure things out for yourself.

After the shattering news at home, I found I always wanted to be around other people: I didn't like to be alone, because then I had time to think about my situation. It was a tough time, all right. When you're that age, it's hard enough dealing with your emotions and life in general without anything else to worry about.

I was very unhappy back at school after that Christmas holiday. On top of my parents' split, it was also my first year at boarding school. Everything seemed wrong, and I decided to do something about it. After a few weeks, this big, bold not-quite twelve-year-old made a momentous decision – he was getting out, escaping. I'm not sure his escape plans had been sufficiently hatched to know exactly where he was going, but he was definitely getting out of there. On the night planned for the escape, I kept myself awake after lights-out in the dormitory. My bags had been quietly packed and were ready at the foot of the bed. I waited until midnight, and on the first strike of the clock, which we could hear in the school, I slipped out of bed. I threw my clothes on within seconds, put on shoes and picked up my bags.

I crept downstairs, fearing the worst every time I heard a floorboard creak, but eventually reached the front door. I was nearly free … until I tried the door and found it locked. Tamely, I crept back up the stairs, put my bags down, climbed back into bed and fell asleep. That was the end of my great escape.

I didn't pick up a rugby ball until I was eight or nine years old. I'd never seen the game until then, at Paarl Boys Primary. At that time, we used to play barefoot, which was a bit bizarre, especially on cold mornings. You would take the first few steps out onto the cold, often wet, fields with the trepidation of someone walking on scalding hot sand. But at least you got used to it after a while.

At that age, we had full-on contact on the field, and I suppose not wearing boots lessened the risk of injury. These games weren't very organised, not unlike a lot of junior school rugby. The fastest boy in the team got the ball and generally ran past everyone else to score. There wasn't much science to it.

But I took to rugby immediately. I really started enjoying the game at ten or eleven, by which time I was playing at No. 8. I scored lots of tries from that position and seemed to get on all right.

For me, rugby was the ideal game. It required a high degree of physicality, which suited me perfectly. At that age, some youngsters held back, but I wasn't one of them. I enjoyed the physical challenge from the start, and I tackled really hard and very well. Later on, I found I caused quite a few serious injuries in schoolboy rugby with my powerful tackling.

Defending and tackling quickly became my strengths in the game. The boys were often too scared to tackle, but I revelled in it. Paarl Boys would meet almost all the big rugby-playing schools of the Cape, such as Rondebosch, Bishops and SACS (South African College School).

Overall, the game gave me something to do, as well as a sense of purpose and identity. When you played well in a team, people congratulated you, and I liked that. I was a wild child, quite fearless, and I think that suited the rugby. I enjoyed the camaraderie, and I really warmed to the team element. Being involved in a team sport seemed to fill a hole in my life. I found the other sports we practised around that time lonely: athletics, and in particular the 200- and 400-metre hurdles, as well as the 50-metre short sprints in swimming.

The first ever trophy I held was for the Craven Week Under 13s, and that was a huge moment. Craven Week, named after the guru of South African rugby, Dr Danie Craven, is when rugby teams from all regions of South Africa come together for one week in the year to compete against each other. The tournament is held at a different venue every year. By coincidence, when I was Under 13, the tournament was held at Paarl Gymnasium, and I was selected for the Western Province Under 13 side. We won the competition, beating Transvaal in the final, and that was my first big victory, holding up that trophy. I think I began to realise then that I could compete with any of the loose forwards in my age group in the country. In short, I could play this game.

They'd probably made me captain because I was the most difficult to control, hoping that a bit of reverse psychology might

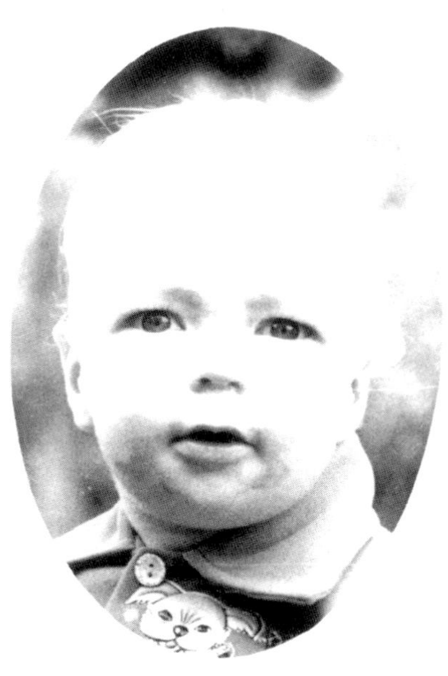

At about twelve months

As a boy in Zambia,
with the daughter of family friends

With the tracker Chorrie and my first buck,
a puku, which is indigenous to Zambia

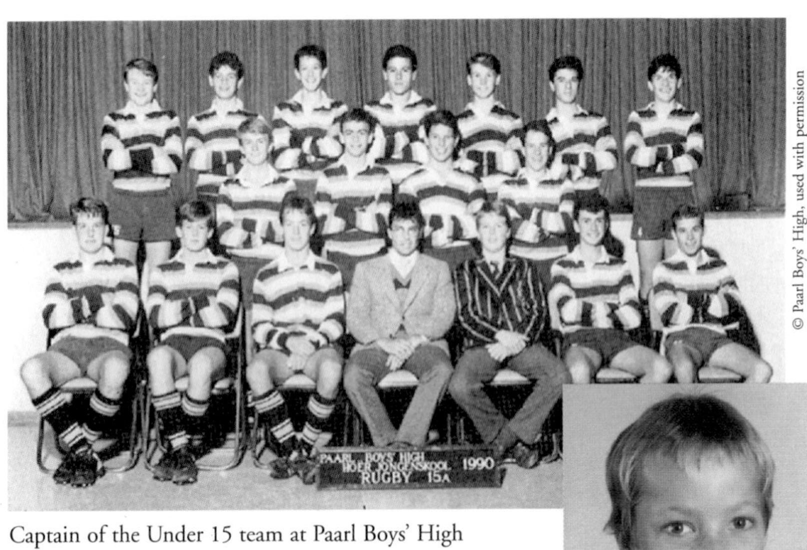

Captain of the Under 15 team at Paarl Boys' High

As a schoolboy at
Paarl Primary

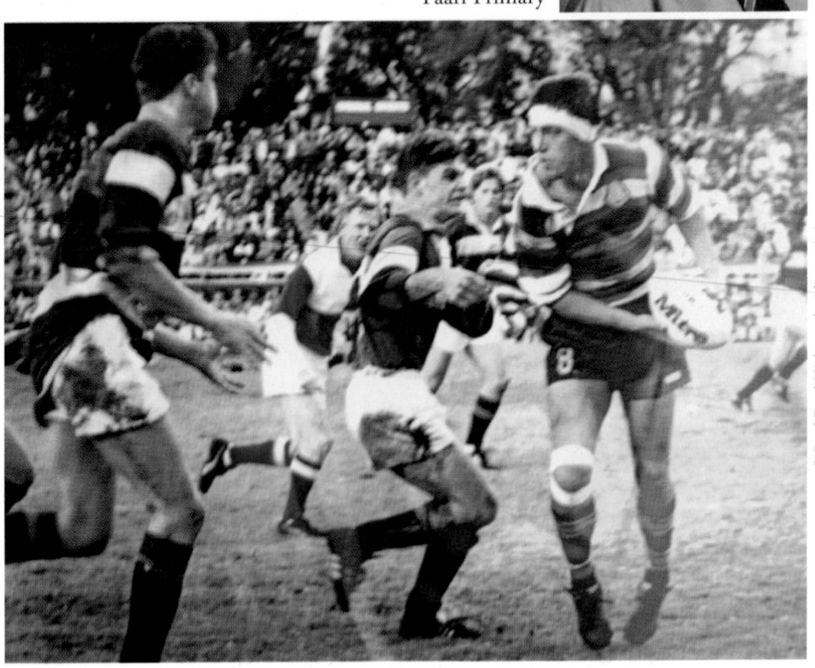

Paarl Boys' High versus Paarl Gym, Inter-schools competition, 1993

The Western Province Under 21 team in 1995, celebrating our Currie Cup win. I am in the second row, dead centre

The WP team in 1996. I am next to Bobby Skinstad, at the top right of the third row

WP trials in February 1997.
Hottie Louw carries the ball, I am on his right

Diving over for a try, May 1997

Currie Cup final against Free State, October 1997. Because of this injury, my first anterior cruciate tear, I would miss the end-of-year Springbok tour

Running onto the field against SWD for
my first game after the car accident, October 1998

On the attack for the Springboks against
the Glasgow Caledonians, 10 November 1998

My debut as Springbok captain in June 1999. Robbie Kempson
and I singing the national anthem. We beat Italy 101-0

With Chester Williams at a training session for a Tri-Nations match against New Zealand in July 2000

Carried off the field after beating the Sharks in the 2000 Currie Cup final

With Breyton Paulse and the Currie Cup

I had fractured a finger only moments before scoring for the Springboks against Ireland at Lansdowne Road, Dublin. We won 28-18

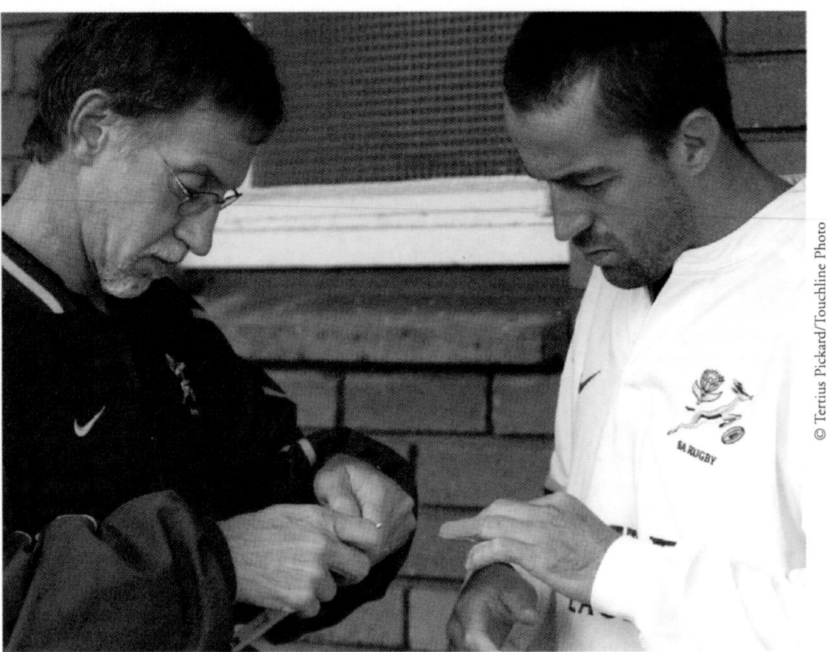

Dr Frans Verster making a splint for the finger I injured against Ireland

work. And it did. Certainly, it meant an awful lot to me to captain a team to such success.

What sort of a captain was 'C Krige' in those days? Well, I was relaxed about off-field discipline, but on the field I was quite hard on the guys. We had school matches most weekends during the season, usually on Saturday mornings, and the season would usually run from March to July. We'd train two or three times a week, and I made sure the guys kept to the timetable. So, too, did one of our masters and tutors, Mr Basson.

I can't say that I went looking for rugby and found it. Rather, it presented itself to me, and I just stumbled into it by starting to play. At Paarl, we were encouraged to play all sorts of sports, although we didn't have football at the school. In summer, there was cricket, but that never appealed to me as a boy. I probably didn't have enough ball sense to play it.

What I liked about rugby was its competitive element and the physical commitment the game required. Competition was always the thing for me in whatever I did. Sometimes it landed me in trouble because I was too competitive – not just in rugby, but in everything. Just a pity I wasn't as deadly competitive when it came to my studies. Frankly, I wasn't great at school. I hated maths but enjoyed geography. You could be taught either in English or Afrikaans, and I was in the English class all the way through until my penultimate year, when I switched to Afrikaans. I'd been taught in English in Zambia, but we spoke Afrikaans at home. So I was fully bilingual, equally comfortable in both languages.

One thing I'd never been comfortable with was boarding at school. However, in 1987, at the age of eleven, soon-to-be twelve, I became a pupil at Paarl Boys High. Perhaps – although I didn't know it at the time – that was what helped me stay on the straight and narrow, on the right side of good and bad. When you go to high school, you go through an initiation. There are certain rules you have to follow, and whatever you may think about them, you find yourself having to adapt. Perhaps I needed those boundaries at that stage of my life.

However, not only was I boarding at the school, but I was one of four or five boys from the junior intake who had to go and board in the senior residence. As the junior residence was overflowing, a small group was selected to go and live in the seniors' block. This meant a lot more than just boarding with the older boys. The next twelve months of our lives would be spent as their 'fags', an initiation process I found very tough at times. But I am convinced it was a good thing in the long term, as it helped knock the rough edges off me. Usually junior pupils had a year to settle in, before undergoing the initiation (or rather, becoming 'fags' for the seniors). But because our little group was in the seniors' residence block in our first year, we got hammered straight away. They say that in adversity you stick together, and François Grobbelaar, Jacques Wege and I grew especially close. We became the best of mates, and are still good friends to this day.

In that year we encountered bullying, big time. Basically, we had to do whatever the seniors told us. For instance, you had to be ball boy when they played table tennis because they were too lazy to go and pick up the ball themselves.

The mornings were a real ritual. I had to get up early, well before my 'boss', as he was called (even though the seniors were only seventeen or eighteen), and make him a cup of tea or coffee before waking him up. Then I had to nip outside his window and make the sound of a dove, so as to wake him up gently. He'd lie in bed and have his tea or coffee, during which time I had to go and sit on the lavatory seat to warm it up for him. When he was ready, he would come into the toilet and take the seat. And, while he was in there, I had to go back into his room, make his bed and study his timetable for the day. I would make a careful note of his lessons and then go through his books on the bedside table, picking out the ones he needed that day. After doing that, I would pack them in his schoolbag, take them to the classroom where his first lesson would be, and leave the bag there. It was the life of a servant.

One of the 'treats' we all looked forward to was leaving the school grounds. This was rarely possible, but it was allowed on Friday afternoons. Then, you'd go into Paarl and, as boys do, chat up some of the girls from a local school. We'd walk around, buy a few things, like sweets, and then perhaps stop at the Spur and order a burger and chips. The trick was, as soon as your food arrived, you gobbled up the chips in record time and took just one bite out of the burger. Then you'd call the waiter over and say, 'Can you warm this up; it's not very hot.' They usually brought the burger back from the kitchen with a fresh pile of chips. The trick rarely failed.

However, if your 'boss' said that you had to stay behind on a Friday afternoon, you had no choice but to obey – and you missed your only chance that week of getting out of school. As compensation, you might be given some ghastly job like cleaning out the fishpond.

My particular 'boss' was called Dirk de Jongh, and he was a really nice guy who was never too demanding. But that didn't mean other seniors couldn't send you out on chores. Generally, I found the whole fag situation pretty demeaning. Some of the seniors tried to break you down because they couldn't cope with the authority they had been given. But you knew you just had to get through it.

One guy was seriously mean, and we were all frightened of him. His nickname was Dac. One day we were walking past the washing line at the back of the schoolhouse, and there was a pair of boots balanced on the line. Jacques Wege, one of our group, flicked the line, and of course the boots went flying. All of which greatly amused a bunch of thirteen-year-olds, until we saw Dac approaching. He'd seen what Jacques had done, and said, 'Those boots were mine.' We knew then we were in for it.

Dac said, 'I'm going to make you feel how those boots felt.'

The washing line was made of steel wire, and we had to stand alongside it and put our noses above the line. Dac then flicked the line, which snapped up into our noses. Our eyes watered, and it was quite painful. But that was the sort of sadistic trick he liked to play.

Dac often used to grab me around the neck just after he'd come out of the smoking room. He stank to high heaven, and I'd be wedged into this stinking mass of clothes, arms and body. I think it's one of the major reasons why, to this day, I hate tobacco smoke.

Whenever Dac or one of the other seniors shouted from their window in the seniors' block, one of us juniors would have to go running. But we saw the opportunity to have some fun with the situation. One day, Dac and most of the other seniors were in town, and we were bored. So we decided to nip into the seniors' homeroom, from where we shouted the word 'Sot', which means slave, out the window. Our friends couldn't see who was doing the shouting, but they knew they'd be in trouble if they ignored it.

I put my arm out of the window and waved, which was what the seniors did sometimes. When the guys saw that, they came running up the stairs immediately. I quickly relayed a message from inside the room to a pal of mine on the outside who was in on the joke. When the first of the juniors came panting up the stairs to answer my call, he was ordered to do fifty push-ups. He was halfway through the set when I sent another message, telling him I wasn't ready for him to start yet. Then I asked my pal to tell the other juniors that Dac had ordered another one of them up. And someone else went through the same procedure. Eventually, I came strolling out of the room, and those of us who were in on the joke collapsed laughing.

Crazy, I suppose, but perhaps it proves that those who are bullied can turn into bullies themselves. In the end, my school years helped me to understand the concept of hierarchy and that, when you have power, you should not abuse it. I understood what it was like to be stuffed around, and I made sure the younger players in any teams I captained didn't feel that way.

One of the few positive things to come out of those tough times was the very good friends I made. And those friendships could be one of the reasons why I went on to captain rugby teams. Friendship forms and builds you as a person.

From the age of fourteen, I started visiting my friends at their homes and meeting their parents. I became very good friends with George van Reenen, and Jacques Wege's parents had a really nice, big house at Bikini Beach in Gordon's Bay. We used to go there on weekends to lie on the beach and swim. We'd borrow his sister's moped and drive around on it, thinking we were really cool!

One day, we got more than we bargained for on that wretched moped. Although we were supposed to wear helmets, we didn't. We'd also conveniently overlooked the fact that we needed a licence to drive the moped. One is also well advised to stop at a traffic light when it is red. We didn't – five times. And one is certainly heading for trouble if the police flag you down to stop, and you don't. We didn't.

I saw what was coming, jumped off the moped and ran for it. But although I got away, I stopped to think and decided there was no way I was going to leave my pal to face the music alone. So I made my way to the police station and, sure enough, there he was. I mumbled to the police that I'd also been on the bike, and that they might be looking for me. The charge list began to add up.

The police called Jacques' mother and asked her to come to the station. When she arrived, there was a huge fuss. She really let rip at us in front of the police, so much so that they clearly thought there would be far more punishment coming our way from her than anything they could dish out. So they gave us a warning and left the punishment to her.

When we got in her car and drove off, she just said, 'You

little buggers, make sure you stay out of trouble in future.' And that was it.

The heat was often overwhelming at the school in summer. There seemed to be a general belief, a sort of unspoken rule, that if the temperature ever reached 45°C, we would be given the day off school. The school is situated in a little valley where the wind doesn't blow. Consequently, there is scorching heat for most of the summer, and that means anything up to eight months of the year. One day the excited cry came that Valhalla had been reached! The thermometer on the school wall recorded a temperature of 45°C. However, just as we were about to down our pens, a surprised teacher looked up. There was, he said sternly, to be no time off just because it was a hot day. The solution to working in school buildings without air conditioning? Easy. Just open the window a bit wider. And thus were our dreams of a day off crushed.

In my Under 14 year, I suffered my first major injury as a rugby player. We were playing Rondebosch in a schools match, and I put in a big tackle, hitting the opponent really hard. Unfortunately, as can sometimes happen in those circumstances, I came off worst. I fell off the boy, feeling a searing pain in my left shoulder. I knew at once I'd done something serious, and had to leave the field. When we got to the hospital, it was confirmed that I had dislocated my shoulder, and would be out for six weeks.

In a sense I was lucky, because throughout my years of playing school rugby, that was the only serious injury I ever suffered.

In my senior year, the fag system was still flourishing. I selected a junior who was almost as big as me to stay in the senior residence, so that he could stand up for himself. I didn't want to bully someone small. I think I was quite tough on him – I wasn't easy. Yet I was always fair. I never asked him to do any of the things I'd hated doing when I was in his position, like making him warm up the toilet seat for me. But if he caused trouble, I would give him a punch in the ribs or something. Yet we always had a good relationship and, in the end, he became a good rugby player as a No. 8.

In the South African schools system of those days, you were Under 14 in Standard 6, Under 15 in Standard 7 and Under 16 in Standard 8. In Standard 9, you played your first year at Under 19, and in your matric year, you were Under 19 for the second year in a row. I was always a year younger than most of those in my group. For example, for Craven Week, when I was in the Under 13s, I was actually not yet twelve, and that continued all the way through my school years.

As I mentioned, at Under 19, the matric guys are in their second year, and so, when my turn came, I decided to go to the headmaster and ask him if I could stay another year. I really wanted to play for the Under 19s at Craven Week, but wasn't sure I would make it in my first Under 19 year.

Towards the end of my penultimate year at school, I saw the headmaster and asked whether I could repeat Standard 9. He asked me why I wanted to stay behind. I said I needed to improve my school results to go to university. My results had not been great – an average of 55 per cent, which was a D. Very average. He agreed, so I did my second year in Standard 9, which meant I had the chance of another year in the Under 19 rugby team, too. As it turned out, the first time I was chosen for the Under 19 side, I was actually still sixteen. I wasn't a big boy, but I was solid, well built and strong. That was partly due to my upbringing on the farm, which toughened me up. Having two older brothers to fight all the time also helped!

That extra year was spent most profitably … on the rugby field. I played a lot of rugby, but didn't study much. I made the Craven Week Under 19 team and the South African Schools B team, the latter for a match against the South African Academy side. But my first big pressure game, as big as a test match (or so it felt at the time) was the local derby: Paarl High against Paarl Gymnasium. That was the big one for the Under 19 team.

The two schools played each other at all sports: golf, hockey, netball and rugby. A crowd of between 12 000 and 15 000 would turn up for that rugby match, played in Paarl at the town sports ground. It was a massive occasion.

The first time I played that match, in 1992, we lost, even though we thought we had a dream team. Louis Koen, who played for Paarl Gym and would also go on to play for the Springboks, kicked us to defeat, by something like 15-20. The following year, when I was captain, we had a kicker at fullback, JC de Klerk, but he'd had an awful season, missing kicks in all our games. However, on the big day we won the derby 19-17, when JC converted a last-minute try from the touchline.

Those were memorable occasions. The first year, I remember crying in the dressing room before the game, from a combination of nerves and excitement. I was so wound up, I just wanted to go out and crush the opposition. But the next year, when I was captain, I realised that one of the reasons why we had lost before was because we had been *too* fired up. So I calmed the players down in the dressing room before the game, and that worked for us.

In 1993, we had a decent scrum that put Paarl Gym under a lot of pressure. Louis Koen also felt a lot of pressure from me that day. Fortunately for us, he didn't have a very good game, and we came out on top. To this day, it remains one of the proudest moments of my life on a rugby field.

My world was quite small at the time. But, probably due to my exploits on the rugby field, I was selected to be head boy of my residence in matric. The head boy of the whole school was also in my residence and everybody thought he'd be appointed head boy of the residence too. But the students chose me, and I must admit, I was chuffed. The teachers knew I could be a bit naughty, but fortunately they thought I was what you might call 'nice naughty'.

On our last school day of 1993, the day before we were to start a study period prior to writing our matric exams, a group of us decided to go down to the beach and have a party. We got into someone's pickup van and headed down to Koel Bay. The all-day party under a hot sun proved thoroughly unwise. In our group was a massive guy who stood about 6 foot 8 inches, called Wium Basson. He later toured with the Springboks on their 1997 tour to Europe. Tragically, he was to die just four years later, from lung cancer.

Anyway, when we arrived at the beach, we saw that we were by no means the only school group to have had the bright idea. Guys from several other schools were also there, and one of them started to irritate Wium. After a few beers, Wium got involved in a fight with the guy and knocked him out. The boy's mates dragged him off and he ended up in the local hospital.

He was unconscious for a few hours, for Wium was one hell of a big guy, and if he hit you and meant it, you knew all about it. But when the boy woke up in a hospital bed, he told his mother, who was anxiously waiting at his bedside, that the Paarl Boys were drinking and fighting on the beach. She phoned our headmaster and told him what had happened.

The order went out from our head to the junior masters to check which boys did not arrive for dinner that night. Unfortunately, we didn't even think about returning to the residence for dinner. The party was going so well on the beach, it didn't enter anyone's head. When we eventually got back, the housemaster was waiting in my room. I had champagne in my hair and must have been reeking of alcohol. And when he said curtly, 'Have you had a good day?' I started giggling – which, in hindsight, was probably not the best thing to do.

So we trooped off to see the headmaster. Of course, word spreads like wildfire in a school about interesting misdemeanours, and I remember walking down the long corridor, with my housemaster, and hands were reaching out from doorways, offering me pieces of chewing gum. I thought the gum might help, until the master, perfectly aware of what was going on, said, 'You can chew as much as you like; you stink so much it will make no difference.'

The heads of the four residences were awaiting my presence in the headmaster's office. It looked like a hanging court already in session. In front of the judges stood the defendant, torn to pieces by the sun, drunk, swaying on his feet despite trying to stand still, and looking and feeling horrible.

The headmaster was extremely angry. He asked me how much I'd had to drink, and I said six beers, hoping he'd be satisfied with that. The truth was, I'd probably consumed double that on the drive to the beach alone. Then we'd had six hours of drinking at the party.

He asked me to tell him about the fight. I felt I couldn't lie, so I told him. I didn't know why Wium had hit the boy. I first knew about it when some other guys came rushing over and said Wium had hit a boy on the chin and knocked him out. When I went to see what it was all about, I got scared, because this guy was lying very still. I left him with his friends and we took Wium off with us, because I was worried he might carry on hitting him. We'd all had far too much to drink.

I was eventually dismissed, and, as I walked out, Wium was outside, looking very nervous, waiting for his turn to be grilled. I said, 'Just tell the truth.'

Back in the residence, the deputy headmaster said he was extremely disappointed in me, and that I'd blown it all with one day of bad behaviour. He told me to report to the headmaster's office in the morning for another meeting.

By the time I got there the next day, the temperature must have been about 38°C. We'd been told to wear full uniform: blazer, tie, trousers, everything. Fifteen of us stood there listening to the head.

It was so hot, one of my friends keeled over, from the combination of a hangover, too little sleep and the fierce heat. He fainted on the spot. The headmaster just ignored him and carried on lecturing us. He told us that if the injured boy did not fully recover, we would all be expelled. I had another three to four weeks left at school at the time, but they threatened to throw me out before I took my matric exams. This was serious stuff.

I felt angry with myself. I'd spent five years trying to impress my teachers, but all of that had gone out of the window in one mad day. I guess in the end I'd shown them that the real me was the wild child. I enjoyed the times when a few of our group would go to a friend's home and drink lots of beer and let our hair down. Deep down, I suspected I wasn't designed to be a teacher's pet, a steady type whom they could always rely on. I just wasn't that person.

And, as we'd progressed through our teens at school, we also discovered girls. In my matric year, I had quite a serious girlfriend, which was another distraction from my studies. I was always living life to the full, leaving things until the last minute, studying through the night in the final weeks and trying to stay awake. I think it's fair to say I was not a dedicated scholar.

In the end, my average went from 55 per cent to 56 per cent. In other words, I scraped through with a D. But a pass is a pass, as a rugby player might say. However, I realise now that not to study properly was a stupid thing to do. And I could probably have spent that extra year at school much more productively at university.

But school did teach me a lot of things about life. Especially about life's unpredictability, its twists and turns. One day, we were playing a game of rugby. One of the players in the opposing team was a kid called Tertius Hickman. He was a year younger than me, but we'd played trials against each other for the Under 19s, and he was quite good. He'd certainly made a bit of a name for himself the year before.

In this match, he was playing very well, and I thought he was being far too cocky for his own good. I ended up punishing him, laying it on the line, in effect putting him in his place. By the end of the game, he was black and blue.

After the final whistle, a man I didn't know came up to me. He was a very short, stocky, strong-looking man. He introduced himself as Thomas Hickman, Tertius's father. My heart sank. I thought, 'Oh, no, here comes a belting if ever I saw one. If this guy gives me one slap, that's the end of me.'

But he put out his hand for me to shake and said, 'I want to thank you for sorting out my son today. He needed someone to give him a hiding like that, or he'd get too big for his boots.' I was unsure of what to say, but that was the start of a long friendship with the Hickman family. To this day, we're still very good friends and they're great people. I spend a lot of time at their home.

When you have written your final exam in matric, it is a long-standing tradition to head off down the coast to Hermanus. Hermanus is perhaps better known as a tourist location for whale watching, but for us, it was a long white beach where all the kids ending their school career could go and chill out, drink beer and have fun. It was as much a gathering place for young people as it was for whales!

I planned to honour this age-old tradition, but Thomas Hickman came to me and said: 'You can stay with us, and go out in Paarl and have a few drinks. But you're not going to Hermanus.' He knew what was likely to happen to me down there, and was looking out for me as a good friend of his son.

Of course, I was upset I couldn't go to Hermanus. But instead I met up with another pal who was finishing that year, Henry Hamman, and we went into Paarl, to have a beer. One turned into several, and it was quite late when we finally got back to Henry's house. The problem was, I'd promised the Hickmans I'd stay with them, and it was quite a long way to their home from Henry's. So Henry gave me his bike at two o'clock in the morning and, slightly the worse for wear, I set off for the Hickmans' home. The road was mainly flat, but there is quite a long hill up to their house on the outskirts of Paarl. I fell off the bike twice trying to get up that hill, but finally made it to the top.

People with outstanding values and kindness, like the Hickmans, were great to spend time with. They reminded me of what good, honest human beings should be like, and how they could help others. In other words, how they could demonstrate the qualities of true Christians.

As kids, we were brought up in the Christian faith, attending church every Sunday. It was always an important part of my life. But in high school, I wasn't always a dedicated Christian, even though I read my Bible, prayed every night and went to church on Sundays. I couldn't always say I was living a Christian life ...

When my parents split up, I did not turn to religion to help me through the situation. I did not think it could help me. But I was only eleven then. Looking back now, I think religion did in fact play a big part in helping me to get through things, helping me to understand that, in the end, things do work out. I was taught that God gives you parents to mould you as a person, but I think it is only recently that I learnt to appreciate that.

My school years had been a time of great highs and plunging lows. I'd experienced personal heartbreak and its accompanying miseries, but also the comfort of very good friends – almost simultaneously, it seemed sometimes. There had been moments of great success and crass failure, but I'd learnt to look after myself and stand on my own two feet. There may have been times, particularly in my younger years, when I hadn't always handled situations all that well. But isn't that what youth and inexperience are all about? Gradually, as I matured, I learnt to be more flexible, less impetuous and a little wiser. I began to think about things in a more sober, mature manner.

In our final year at school, we had to decide what future subjects we wanted to study, and which college or university we wanted to attend. Most people go from Paarl to Stellenbosch

University, but I didn't want to do that. I was quite well known in that small pond in my own circles, and felt that it would be better to break out and make a fresh start in the far bigger pond of Cape Town. I needed to go to the big city. A lot of my close friends went on to Stellenbosch, which meant that, when I got to Cape Town, I had to take responsibility and fight my own battles. Luckily, I was already well used to that.

Today, I probably regret going to Cape Town – it would have been fun to spend more time with my friends from schooldays. But at the time it seemed like the right choice, especially as the Cape Technikon had offered me a bursary.

I signed up for a retail business management course, which was spread over three years, from 1994 to 1996. It seemed ideal while I played rugby.

But before I'd really settled in at Tech, rugby football seized centre stage in my life. I was chosen to captain the South African Under 19 side at the World Cup in France in 1994. It promised to be a great trip and a huge challenge, and you'd have recognised me easily enough as we prepared to leave South Africa on a flight to Paris. I was the one eagerly bounding up the steps onto the aeroplane. A whole new adventure was awaiting my team and me.

4
A Whole New Adventure

There was a very particular reason why my teammates and I were able to wing our way to the Under 19 Rugby World Cup in France in 1994. A few years earlier, on 11 February 1990, a great event had occurred in the history of South Africa. Nelson Mandela finally walked free after almost twenty-eight years of imprisonment, heralding a new beginning after years of apartheid.

I was only fourteen that day, but I still remember Mandela's statesmanship, his elegant gait and calm demeanour as he walked out of prison, hand in hand with his then wife, Winnie.

Not everyone was ecstatic at this turn of events. A lot of people had wondered what would happen if Mandela was released. Many thought there would be anarchy, and a lot of whites were even stockpiling food, making sure they would have enough supplies to survive for at least a few weeks. It was a time of huge uncertainty.

Apartheid had polarised opinions in our country. Some white people feared that if black people were given the vote, there would be certain bloodshed aimed at the whites. It may sound dramatic now, but for years white South Africans had been indoctrinated to believe that Nelson Mandela was a terrorist, and if he were ever released, he and his colleagues would resume their nefarious activities. The apartheid government based their arguments on fear, and to a large extent it worked.

I was always comfortable in the presence of black people, because of the way I'd grown up on the farm in Zambia. In my eyes, black people were no different from me. Yes, the adults were our servants, but their kids were our friends, and we treated them the same way we'd treat our white friends. But when I arrived in South Africa as a seven-year-old, I began to realise that the system here was very different. Consequently, when the time came for change, I never had trouble adapting, unlike a lot of white South Africans.

Only once in my life have I ever been accused of being a racist, and it made me so angry, I was very glad there were other people near me at the time, or I might have inflicted serious harm on the person who had made the unwarranted accusation. It happened during a Stormers Super 12 tour of Australasia, at one of those light-hearted sessions when players and officials get hauled up in front of a 'court' and accused of all sorts of nonsensical offences. It is supposed to add some fun to the trip and turn the focus away from non-stop rugby. But it went very wrong on this particular occasion.

One of our black managers, Derrick Peterson, was 'arraigned' on some arbitrary charge and, predictably, found guilty. His sentence was to down alcohol, but as he didn't drink, I changed the sentence to downing high-energy sports drinks. He drank about three and a half litres of the stuff during the run of the evening, and a lot of the black guys in our squad, like Wayne Julies and Bolla Conradie, were giving him a lot of lip. Peterson became very angry and upset. In the corridor outside the hotel room, he took me aside and called me a racist. He was so angry that he even said he was ready to fight me. He then stuck his finger under my nose in a thoroughly provocative manner.

It was fortunate that I was in total control of myself, or I might have knocked him out, as I was extremely angry. I told him I had grown up with black people, had gone to school with them and had black friends, so I never wanted to be a called a racist again. Our coach, Gert Smal, heard the commotion and broke it up, but I was very upset. People can call me a lot of things, but never a racist. No one else has ever done so, except Derrick Peterson.

After I laid a complaint with the Western Province Rugby Union CEO, Rob Wagner, Peterson became a manager at one of the other South African teams.

But, in 1994, as momentous events in the history of South Africa were unfolding, including the first democratic election on 27 April, South African sport was beginning to enjoy the fruits of Nelson Mandela's release and the ending of the apartheid era. Our sports teams, denied international competition for many years, had been welcomed back into the fold in 1992. In October 1994, a new-look South African rugby team set off for an overseas tour to the United Kingdom. The party, managed by Jannie Engelbrecht and captained by François Pienaar, played thirteen matches in Wales and Scotland, losing only to Scotland A and finally to the Barbarians, in Dublin. More importantly, that team would form the core of the South African World Cup–winning team that would beat New Zealand in the final to lift the William Webb Ellis Trophy eight months later. Players such as Chester Williams, André Joubert, Japie Mulder, Joel Stransky and Joost van der Westhuizen were among the backs, and up front were Os du Randt, Balie Swart, Kobus Wiese, Mark Andrews and Ruben Kruger.

But also taking place that year was the Under 19 Rugby World Cup in France. The tournament was based in Lyon, in the central south-east of France, the city on the mighty Rhône River known for its gastronomic delights. By that time I had already been out of school for a year, but still qualified to play Under 19. I was also made captain, which I regarded as a great honour.

But this being Under 19 level and still officially in the old amateur era (professionalism was banging hard on the door and would be brought in the following year), the arrangements were indeed a trifle amateurish. After we met up in Johannesburg and flew to Paris, we had to get from Charles de Gaulle Airport in the north of the city to the railway station on the east side, from where the high-speed TGV trains departed for Lyon. Imagine a whole rugby squad, complete with personal luggage, tackle bags and rugby kit, unloading the whole lot at a Paris Métro station, and carrying it all up the escalators and stairs. It was chaotic.

We had been given blazers with the Springbok emblem on the left breast pocket, but we didn't have an anthem to sing when the time came. Our old anthem was very closely associated with the apartheid era and was no longer used. The newly elected government was working on a new anthem and flag. So, when we lined up for the anthems before each game we played, the opposition's anthem was played while we had a minute's silence instead of ours. It was quite bizarre.

The joy of the tour was that it was a fully integrated South African squad, blacks, whites and coloureds. At the beginning of the trip, it was a bit difficult to integrate, but after that we all mixed happily, and created a very good team spirit. The black players taught the rest of us a lot of their songs, which we then sang throughout the trip. Out of the thirty players in the squad, I seem to remember there were five or six black guys. Not many by today's standards, but this was still early days in the dawn of the new South Africa.

We worked our way steadily through the tournament, beating teams like France and Ireland, and meeting Argentina in the semi-final. They were so emotional they were crying on the field before the kick-off, so we knew it was not going to be an easy ride.

Our side was very young and inexperienced – some of our guys were still at school. But there was plenty of quality in future Springboks such as Louis Koen and Faan Rautenbach, who would later play tight head for the Boks.

We reached the end of the semi-final in the lead, having defended really well, and prepared to celebrate going into the final. But little did we know that the referee was going to play a ludicrous amount of extra time – almost ten minutes! We were just hanging on, trying to contain the increasingly desperate Argentinians and tackling anything that moved. Our coach, Spiere van Rensburg, was going absolutely potty on the touchline, and no wonder. I knew I had to keep cool and handle the referee wisely, or it could have gone against us. But today I can say that he had been absolutely diabolical, and could have cost us the game.

But in the end, we heard the final whistle with a mixture of elation and relief. We were through to the final, where we beat Italy in a rather one-sided game. We were the world champions!

And, the following year, so were the Springboks. Every South African rugby fan will always remember 1995 with pride. To see our country win the World Cup the first time we were permitted to play for it was a remarkable moment, highlighted by watching Nelson Mandela present the trophy to François Pienaar while wearing a Springbok jersey. If ever there was a true act of reconciliation for a nation after years of division, that was surely it. Millions around the world must have retained within their memory the sight of this gentle, elegant man wearing a Springbok rugby shirt and presenting Pienaar with the World Cup.

I remember training with the Western Province Under 21 team on 25 May 1995, the day of the opening game of the World Cup. Australia, the holders, played against South Africa, the host nation, and the Springboks won 27-18 at a packed Newlands. I had been keen to go and see the game, but we couldn't, as we were training. But I followed all the World Cup games very closely.

Initially, there seemed to be a general feeling among South African rugby followers that, yes, they supported the team, but first let's see how they do before we get too carried away. This is typical of South African rugby fans. But once the momentum built, they were right behind the team and the support swelled. There was a great atmosphere throughout the country and a real buzz because of the rugby. When the Springboks beat New Zealand in the final at Ellis Park, Johannesburg, I was in Cape Town, watching the game on television. Afterwards, flags were flying everywhere in the city. People were hanging out of the windows of apartment blocks, and winning the cup proved to be a massive unifying event for the entire country. To see black and white people dancing together in the streets so soon after the end of apartheid was simply unbelievable.

As South Africa proved at the time, sport can be a thoroughly unifying force. People either unite in joy when their team succeeds or unite in collective grief when things go wrong. But, personally, I don't think sport should be used to try to unify people. The fact is, if you leave sport alone and allow it to do what it does best – entertain – it will unite people anyway. Different people from different cultures will integrate under one banner where sport is involved. It comes naturally.

Not only was it heartening that black and white came together at the time, but many conservative South Africans also realised that moving the country forward was a good thing for all the people of the land. However, I don't believe the World Cup would have had such an effect if we had lost! Yet it seemed inevitable that the special spirit from that time was going to dissipate at some stage. It is probably understandable. But it is unfortunate that no one built on the success of that tournament. Instead, we relaxed and rested on our laurels.

It was a wonder I managed to do any work at the Cape Technikon, as rugby was steadily taking over my life. And, in fact, in the end I left college after only two of the three years of the scheduled course, departing without sitting my final exams. But I didn't feel it mattered. I'd been away in France for several weeks at the Under 19 World Cup in 1994, and the following year Western Province won the Under 21 championships, hammering Free State in the final in Bloemfontein. Every single member of that team went on to play provincial rugby, and most of us would go on to play international rugby in the future. People like Percy Montgomery, Robbie Fleck, Louis Koen, Selborne Boome, Hottie Louw and Dave van Hoesslin were destined to move through the ranks of Western Province rugby with great success.

Those players who were young enough could play for two or

three years at Under 21 level. We played our matches as curtain-raisers at Newlands to Western Province's Currie Cup games. We'd get around 3 000 to 5 000 supporters to see us. Anyone talent-spotting from Newlands's towering stands at that time would have had a rich harvest on which to feast. We played a very exciting type of game, running from everywhere, and as people started to hear about our brand of rugby, our support grew.

I remember something very specific about that Under 21 season, and especially the final in Bloemfontein. We were paid R250 a game, and the money was given to you in an envelope, in cash, before the match. But after winning the final, we each received an envelope with R1 000 in cash. That was a massive amount of money in those days for so-called, er, amateur players! But, of course, everyone knew that the barriers concerning payment of players were being dismantled at a rapid pace. Everyone, it seemed, except some of the unions up in the northern hemisphere, like England, which were caught unawares when the International Rugby Board, at their meeting in Paris in August 1995, announced that the game would henceforth be open. In other words, professionalism had arrived.

The Western Province side was known as a party team: it was a 'work hard, play hard' type of mentality. We were unbeaten through that season, and when we won the final, we each took R350 of our winnings and said we wouldn't be going home until we'd finished off the money celebrating. We had a huge party that night, which was a shade unfortunate, as our coach, Piet Faasen, was a very conservative man who hated the fact that we would drink so much after games. Some of the boys weren't averse to swearing either, and Piet abhorred bad language.

At one stage that night I remember Robbie Fleck, Percy Montgomery and me play-fighting outside the lift in the team hotel. In fact, the pair of them were wrestling with me on the ground, and Robbie was shouting, 'You don't mess with us, Englishman!' I was laughing my head off, but I suppose it looked a bit unseemly.

Suddenly, they let me go, and I sat up to be confronted by the sight of our coach, standing in the passageway, saying, 'I think you need to go to bed.'

We did, meekly.

Unfortunately, rugby teams and hotels don't always get along too well, a fact that was underlined the next morning. When I came out of my room to go down to breakfast, I saw that a large sign was missing from the wall next to the lift. I was sure it had been there the day before, and I feared the worst. Somehow, I just knew one of us had removed it. As it turned out, someone had ripped it off the wall, but I knew we would all be in trouble if our coach found out what had happened. So I knocked on everyone's door, waking most of them up, and demanded to know who had taken the sign and where it was now.

I'd have said the most unlikely person to have the sign was our scrumhalf, Dave von Hoesslin. I woke him up, got him to the door and explained my plight. 'Oh, it's under my bed,' he said, very matter-of-factly.

By this time, I'd also discovered that our coach was downstairs, having breakfast. So I called the hotel's maintenance guy, told him I needed help with something, and, when he arrived on our floor, we managed to put the metal plate back on the wall. Then, after he left, I watched from my room, which had a view of the wall.

Out of the lift stepped Piet Faasen. He walked past the wall in question, did a double take and came back, peering closely at the sign to see how it had been fixed up. After a moment, he just shook his head and walked on.

We had a very talented team, but also a very naughty one. We didn't need any invitations to go out and enjoy ourselves. And we certainly enjoyed ourselves both on and off the field, playing with the carefree attitude of kids in the park. There was no tension before a game, because we knew that we just had to play to our potential and we would win. We had the ability to beat any side as long as we didn't underestimate them. But I do remember one game we nearly lost to Eastern Province. I think anyone could tell we weren't focusing properly: we'd all shaved off most of our hair the day before.

In 1996, I made the Western Province 1st XV for the first time. It was considered a singular honour and a very special moment to go into the dressing room at Newlands and pull on the senior WP rugby jersey with those famous blue and white stripes. I'll never forget the feeling: a mixture of pride and determination to succeed. I knew the years ahead would be tough, because South African rugby was tough. But that didn't deter me in the slightest – the harder it was, the better I liked the challenge. I had always played at No. 8 during my school days, but when I played for Gardens Tech and at Western Province, they suggested I move to the flank. I probably wasn't tall enough to play No. 8 in senior rugby, and besides, Western Province had a superb player in that position already. His name was Tiaan Strauss, and he was the main man in the WP pack. He also happened to be my hero. I thought I would love to be like him. He was an honest, hard-working guy. He didn't seem very flashy, always looked quite humble and he was a superb player. You could see his power, his ball-handling skills, his positional play and how he motivated his teammates. But eventually he left Cape Town for a new life in Australia. In the years ahead, I would play against Tiaan in the Super 12 competition, when he represented the New South Wales Waratahs and I was playing for the Stormers.

I also made my debut in Super 12 rugby in 1996. I was twenty-one, young for a South African to be in Super 12, though not for an Australian. After all, the Australian wing Ben Tune first played test match rugby at nineteen. I am intrigued by that trait of Australian society. The nation seems to invest in youth at the earliest possible moment, in so many fields. They are not scared to give youngsters a go, reasoning that if they swim rather than sink, they may well have unearthed what they like to call 'a good 'un' for several years to come. I must admit that I like that approach. It challenges a young player. It says to him, 'Okay, you think you're good enough, now prove it.' I see nothing wrong in that. Of course some will fall by the wayside under such a policy, but many will – and do – rise to the challenge, to the long-term benefit of both the country and the sport. I sometimes wish we were more adventurous in that respect in South Africa. Personally, I have always believed in the creed: 'If you're good enough, you're old enough.'

When I played my first season of Super 12, I really didn't know what to expect. I found it physically tough at first, but it is amazing how quickly you adapt. When you play against a side like the Blue Bulls, which included tough players such as lock Johan Ackermann, or Natal, with Mark Andrews, you have to learn quickly. The initiation is short and not terribly sweet. If I'd had any doubts about how harsh this new world would be from a physical point of view, then they disappeared the first time one of those huge guys cleaned me out at a ruck. That was an experience to remember. For several days, actually.

I was never supposed to play Super 12 so early. We'd had trials, but I didn't have a very good game and wasn't originally selected in the starting line-up. But someone got injured and I was called in. It was a wonder I ever bothered returning the call to find out what it was all about.

I was at Cape Technikon in digs when the Western Province coach Alan Zondagh phoned me up to ask me to join the squad. This was the year before Western Province would change their name to the Western Stormers for the Super 12 competition. In 1998, the name would change once again, to the Stormers. I wasn't in to take Alan's call, and someone else answered the phone. When I got back to my room, a message had been pushed under the door saying, 'Please phone Ellen Zombag.'

Ellen Zombag? I knew no such name. But by a process of elimination, I managed to figure out who it was, and thought

I'd better ring just in case it was Alan. I went to training the next day, and discovered that I was in the side to take on the Bulls in a warm-up game. I must have done okay, because I stayed in the side for the match against Natal in Durban, which was our first game that season. We lost that opener 22-28, but I managed to keep my place in the team. But the next match was something else: the New South Wales Waratahs in Cape Town.

This was the stuff of schoolboy fantasy as far as I was concerned. Players like Willie Ofahengaue and David Campese were playing for NSW, there were 40 000 spectators – and this was just my second game in Super 12 rugby. During the match I put in a massive tackle on 'Campo', to see how my hero would handle that. He ran towards me with the ball, did his trademark goose-step, and I thought, I'm not falling for that one, mate. As soon as he stepped inside, I hit him, very hard. I really cleaned him out. But he was all right; he got up fine.

Again, as in Durban, we scored 22 points, but unfortunately New South Wales got 30. After the game, I was far too shy to go up to the great Campese and start a conversation with him. So I just gawped across the room, as youngsters tend to do. Daft, but I couldn't help it. I was young and shy.

I found that the Super 12 was a red-hot mixture of pace and physicality. It is really quick, the fastest competition I ever played in. I don't believe anything gets much faster than that, and you really have to be in peak condition to handle the pace. I wasn't as fit then as later on, and I quickly realised I needed to step up my strength and fitness training. Because, even then, at that young age, I wasn't happy just to compete: I really wanted to dominate my opponents on the rugby field.

Super 12 didn't intimidate me, although I knew it was a significant step up. I was confident I could negotiate that level. It also didn't bother me going into a team that wasn't winning very often. Playing Super 12 rugby was more than I had expected to achieve that season, so I was quite happy. But I was soon to learn all about the difficulties that can arise at the top level of rugby.

In the course of just twelve days, from 22 March to 3 April, we were presented with a playing schedule that read as follows:

22 March: Canterbury (in Christchurch) Drew 16-16;

27 March: Auckland (in Auckland) Lost 30-48;

30 March: Waikato (in Hamilton) Lost 17-44;

3 April: Queensland (in Brisbane) Lost 26-36.

And then, on 10 April, Otago came to Cape Town and beat us 52-25, a humbling, chastening experience.

To this day, I doubt whether I've faced a more absurd schedule. To play Super 12 games of that intensity, you need at least a whole week off between them. And that is only enough if you are playing every game in one location. We went from South Africa to Christchurch, via Auckland; then back to Auckland, then down to Hamilton and then back across the Tasman Sea to Brisbane. In just twelve days!

I managed to last out three of those games until things went disastrously wrong for me against Waikato. One of their players was so far offside it was ridiculous. He caught our scrumhalf at the base of the scrum on our side, when the ball was still among the pack. He was also holding onto me, and then he fell down, blocking the path for the ball to escape on our side. That did it for me. I tried to ruck him, but ended up kicking him in the head. Predictably, after the game, I was cited for the offence and banned for three weeks.

Everyone reacts differently in that type of incident. The Waikato player knew what he was doing, and I'd had enough of him. But it is the scale of the reaction that varies. It is inevitable that people do react. You are put into that kind of situation and things happen very quickly. You don't have ten seconds to think through what you are going to do, or to consider what your options are. Generally, you do the first thing that comes into your head. Then it's too late to stop. I don't believe there is an easy solution to that sort of thing; it's just rugby. But I would be the first to say that you need players who can control their physicality and keep a lid on it. It's as well to remember that part of rugby is being aggressive within the law, and you don't want people to be a liability. Which, I must admit, I was on occasion during my career.

All I can say in my defence is that it's very easy to get caught up in the heat of the moment. How you react probably depends on your personality. If you're like me, it is very easy to go over the top. In the old days of amateur rugby, it was a whole lot easier to get away with things. I'd say congratulations to anyone who could play right on the edge, or still does today, without being busted for foul play. It is an extremely difficult thing to do, particularly during the professional era.

When something like the Waikato incident happened, I usually learnt a lesson. But of course, that lesson would wear off in time, and I made similar mistakes again later on in my career.

At times I struggled with the conflict I felt between grinding people on the rugby field and my religious beliefs. When I overstepped the mark, I was very aware that I was not following the teachings of my religion and was setting a poor example. On the one hand, I was physically hurting people, and on the other I would try to adhere to the teachings of the Bible, which preaches a contrary message. I knew that I was involved in a physical sport. That in itself was okay. But when I did something stupid and lost my temper, I struggled to handle the inner consequences of my actions. Somehow, I felt I had let God down and I felt disappointed in myself, and also embarrassed.

I told myself that if I wanted to be a Christian and lead a Christian life, I couldn't be doing those sorts of things – especially not in front of millions of people on TV! It wasn't the kind of example I wanted to set, and yet, when I ran out onto the field, I sometimes found myself caught up in situations I later regretted. That troubled me. I have never taken my religion lightly. As I've mentioned, my brothers and I were brought up with a strong religious background, and it soon became an important part of our make-up. Trying to equate the teachings of God – looking out for and caring about your fellow man – and some of the things I did on the rugby field against opponents, was a dichotomy to me. It troubled me then, and it still troubles me now when I think about it.

But the problem was, I quickly came to realise that top-class rugby was played on the edge the whole time. There can be no hanging back, no refinement to it. It just isn't that type of game. In rugby, particularly at the highest level, you are often provoked. Early on in my career, especially, I was a bit of a hothead. If the situation called for it, I would not hesitate to climb into someone. But then I started to reason with myself, comparing my religious views with some of the things I did on the rugby field, and I tried to make different decisions than I would have made before. But it wasn't easy.

In a split second – especially when you have been provoked – it is extremely hard not to react. It was particularly hard to justify my actions when I waited to retaliate against a player who had provoked me. I don't remember reading anything in the Bible that says it is acceptable to bide your time and wait to dish out revenge attacks on other human beings. Yet there I was, sometimes doing just that, because I had to wait for the right moment to punch someone who had attacked me. An eye for an eye? Well, maybe.

Now, when I consider this complicated issue, I think God is forgiving and always looks at your heart. I don't believe He wields a big stick, waiting to smack you. But I do think he expects contrition on the part of the sinner, and, quite honestly, there were many occasions when I felt very contrite. I knew when I was in the wrong, and I genuinely regretted it afterwards.

Twickenham 2002, which I will come to later in this book, is a classic case in point. During my time with Northampton, I talked to Cobus Visagie, a great man of South African rugby and also a man of religion, about this conundrum. He gave me something to think about after a match in which he played for Saracens, and I for the Northampton Saints.

Saracens' scrum had shoved us over our own line. The scrum collapsed and I lay there in a heap with my teammates. I looked up and saw Cobus standing over me, with a big grin spread across his face, like the little boy who'd just found the cookie jar in the cupboard. I couldn't resist it; I kicked him hard in the shins, and he fell over. Yet, when we talked about the incident later, he said that, as a Christian, he felt very bad about the way he'd stood there, grinning – taunting me, if you like.

Another time, I played in a game against another former Springbok international, André Vos. He was trying to reach the ball, but was clearly on the wrong side of the maul. So I cleaned him out, hit him hard, and down he went. He was hurt, too.

When he finally got up, he came up to me, looked at me intently and said, 'Corné, why did you do that?' And then, as if answering his own question, he said, as much to himself as to me, 'A leopard never changes its spots, eh?'

Whenever I did something like that, I felt I was failing in my Christian beliefs. It was a contradiction that I carried with me until the day I retired from rugby football.

The final league table in that first Super 12 season I played, in 1996, confirmed my suspicion that we were well off the pace. We finished second to last (Canterbury Crusaders were bottom), with only three wins and one draw from eleven matches.

Such modest form that season cost our coach Alan Zondagh his job. He was sacked, and replaced by Harry Viljoen. I found Harry quite an aggressive figure. He'd been very successful in business, and he certainly knew how to market himself and what he wanted to achieve.

But from my point of view, I was pretty satisfied with the 1996 season. At least I'd played my first really big game at Newlands, and what an experience that had been. The atmosphere and pressure were quite awesome. Newlands is a very personal stadium because the supporters are so close to the field. I always liked that. Newlands had always been close to my heart, and, as the years and big occasions came and went, that special feeling – a love affair, I suppose you could call it – grew even more intense.

Western Province had some tidy performers around that time, powerful players such as Gary Pagel, Fritz van Heerden, Keith Andrews and Christian Stewart. But we didn't have the quality required to match the likes of Auckland, with their cluster of All Blacks, who won the Super 12 in 1996 and 1997.

But in that 1996 season we were steadily building a Western Province team to launch a major challenge for the Currie Cup, which, of course, had always been South Africa's No. 1 domestic trophy. We weren't good enough that year, losing 22-56 in the quarter-finals to a Transvaal team led by François Pienaar, South Africa's World Cup–winning captain. Failing to reach the last four in the Currie Cup meant we missed out on qualifying for the 1997 Super 12. However, not even Pienaar could inspire Transvaal sufficiently to win the Currie Cup. Natal, who had also reached the Super 12 final that year, losing 21-45 to Auckland, took the Currie Cup with a 33-15 victory at Ellis Park.

But this had been an exciting season in general for southern hemisphere rugby. The first Tri-Nations series, the annual competition between South Africa, New Zealand and Australia, had also taken place. The All Blacks not only won that first Tri-Nations title by finishing with a 100 per cent record, but they also made a tour to South Africa that year, winning the test series 3-1, thus becoming the first ever New Zealand side to take a series on South African soil. It was a mighty achievement by their coach, John Hart, and captain Sean Fitzpatrick – and sweet revenge for their loss in the World Cup final the year before.

But, while the senior South African side was losing that series to the All Blacks, a South African 'A' squad was planning to depart on a tour to the UK. I was selected, and we had an enjoyable time. It was the last of those long tours – eight weeks in all – but it was a fascinating experience to spend so much time overseas, playing rugby against similar teams from England, Wales, Scotland and Ireland, as well as playing midweek matches at places like Oxford and Cambridge.

We had a good year at Western Province in 1997. New players, such as James Small and Dick Muir from Natal, had been signed to reinforce the team. Dick was a good leader; James wasn't. In fact, he was a bit of a nutter! But he helped sell the tickets. At the end of May 1997, Western Province pushed the British Lions reasonably hard at Newlands, before going down 21-38.

Eventually WP finished top of the Currie Cup log, winning twelve out of thirteen games, and qualifying for a semi-final against the fourth-placed team, the Gauteng Lions. We'd finished the league programme 13 points ahead of the Lions, but I don't think anyone could have anticipated the result of our meeting in the semi-final. We beat them 88-18, an extraordinary performance full of superb attacking rugby. You could tell the extent of our determination and desire simply by the score. Some teams get on top in a one-sided match, run up 40 to 50 points, and just ease off. That wasn't our style, and besides, we were enjoying ourselves too much to pull back. In the other semi-final, the Free State Cheetahs beat Natal, the defending champions, 38-22, which set up a Western Province–Free State final.

In this game, there was to be no runaway cricket score. In fact, it turned out to be a real battle, but in the end we edged it 14-12 – a try and three penalty goals to four penalty goals. Louis Koen kicked our goals, and Jannie de Beer landed all four for the Cheetahs. The difference was the only try of the match, scored for us by wing Justin Swart. It was, as the experienced and much respected South African rugby writer Dan Retief wrote, 'Western Province's long-overdue return to prominence'. But for me, personally, victory came at a huge price in that final.

I went into the game on a high in three respects: not only was this going to be my first ever Currie Cup final, but it was being played on my home ground, Newlands. And just a few days earlier I had been told I was in the Springbok squad for the end-of-year tour to Europe, which would depart not long after the final.

Nick Mallett had recently been given the job of reviving Springbok rugby after an alarming period in which the Boks lost not one, but two, coaches in no time at all. André Markgraaff had been forced to resign following the revelation of a tape on which he'd made racist remarks about certain administrators in South African rugby. Carel du Plessis replaced him, but he immediately presided over a losing series against the British Lions. Later that same year, in the Tri-Nations, the Boks were thrashed 35-55 by New Zealand in Auckland, and 20-32 by Australia in Brisbane. Anyone who knows anything about the importance of South Africa–New Zealand test matches in our rugby history would understand that a 55-point defeat was not just conclusive – it was shattering.

Ironically enough, when the Australians played the return match of that year's Tri-Nations series in Pretoria, they too were wiped away. The Boks thrashed them 61-22. But not even that beating could eradicate the memory of the humiliation in Auckland, and Du Plessis lost his job.

Into the breach stepped Nick Mallett, just in time to select a squad for the Springboks' end-of-year tour to Italy, France, England and Scotland. Joy of joys, I had been included. I couldn't believe it. But first there was a Currie Cup final to be played and won. We did that, but, sadly, I never finished the game.

I made loads of hard tackles in that final, and got up after every one. But then Chris Badenhorst, the Free State wing, stepped me. Suddenly, I was going the wrong way and, as you do, I tried to stop my momentum and go into reverse gear in one split second. But my leg was in a bad position and I collapsed, clutching my knee. I knew at once I'd done something very serious, and after being carried off the field and taken to see a specialist, I was given the diagnosis I had feared. I had wrecked the anterior cruciate in my right knee, my first big injury. I was told that I would be out of rugby for at least six months.

I was not only in shock, but also pain. The two were a thoroughly unpleasant combination, and I was gutted. The week before, when I'd heard about my selection for the Springboks, I'd been on top of the world. Now, one week later, here I was, down in the dumps.

Rugby, as I came to learn, has the ability to do that to you in all kinds of ways. You can be catapulted to the dizzy heights by a superb win one week, but, just seven days later, find yourself tumbling down after an inexplicable defeat. And very often there appears to be no reason for such a dramatic change of fortune. Your team can play superbly in one match, but appear as though it has never turned up in the next. Players who at one moment looked like world-beaters would suddenly appear as though they just can't play. They drop simple passes, miss easy kicks and allow opponents to run through them to score, whereas in their last match, they might have defended with their lives, never offering the opposition the smallest of gaps. I confess I found that situation bewildering throughout my career, so I can only guess what the coaches of those teams would have been feeling, sitting helplessly on the sideline.

That is the major reason why I will never become a rugby coach. The players will spend the whole week in the build-up to a match kicking every ball, catching every pass and taking every lineout ball. As coach, you will go through your team selection over and over again, questioning whether you have chosen the right men, or got the right combinations to trouble the opponents and do the job. And then, after all that, when your side goes out to play on the day of the match, for some quite unfathomable reason, they just don't play. Why not? No one really knows. It's not as if they're failing deliberately. The players have put as much into the build-up as the coach. But, for whatever reason, the magic doesn't happen, and you lose. I'd find that sort of situation maddening. It was bad enough to experience it as a player, but at least then you could study your play after a defeat and go through the areas where you failed, what you hadn't done right and where your teammates had been below par. But for the poor old coach, he just has to sit and watch it all go wrong. How much pleasure can that give a man?

As my career unfolded, I realised more and more that you never know what life has in store for you. Because what happened to me next threatened to end my career completely – before I'd ever worn a Springbok jersey.

5
Another Day, Another Injury

The road from Malmesbury to Paarl traverses an arid landscape. Towering, rocky crags peer down in intimidating fashion on the small vehicles climbing up the long valley roads. The ground is parched for much of the year, due to the Western Cape's long, hot summers.

Malmesbury is at the heart of South Africa's wheat industry. It's the country's leading wheat distributor and houses one of the biggest flourmills anywhere in the land. It seems as if wheat fields surround the town; whichever way you drive towards it, you see endless fields of wheat gently swaying in the hot breezes that blow in this part of the world. The town lies in what is known as the Swartland, the black country. That term relates chiefly to the soil, but also to a local shrub called the renosterbush, which turns a dark colour in winter.

I'd missed the 1998 Super 12 season because of the serious knee injury I'd sustained in the previous year's Currie Cup final. I'd had the best medical care, and Western Province had looked after me superbly. But only a fool would rush back from such a major injury, and although I was anxious to play as soon as possible, even I wasn't prepared to shorten my recovery period and risk doing further damage. When you sustain bad injuries as a sportsman, you quickly learn to let time take its course, no matter how competitive you are. The experts will give you an estimate of the duration of the healing process, and it isn't just guesswork. They could sometimes be out by a couple of weeks one way or the other, and there's always the chance you will be back earlier than expected, but you certainly don't take risks or shortcuts; that would be stupid.

But by early winter 1998, I was playing again. I had been back in training for some time, taking it very slowly, but eventually regaining full fitness. Not long after, I was travelling from a friend's farm outside Malmesbury towards Paarl. I was driving a pickup, which we'd used to go out hunting the night before. We hadn't slept much, and I was tired and finding concentration difficult. It was warm. I wasn't too worried, as usually there wasn't much traffic on that road, and this particular day had seemed no exception.

But suddenly, right there in front of me, in the middle of the road, was a stationary car. I swerved to miss it, and the violent movement flipped the pickup. It rolled over six or seven times, left the road, went over a farm fence and came to a standstill in a field.

The strangest thing of all was that I'd driven the whole way to Malmesbury not wearing a seat belt. But just before reaching the town, a sign next to the road reminds drivers to wear their seat belts. I remember looking at the sign and thinking I'd better put it on. Not even ten kilometres later, I crashed. Had I not been wearing that seat belt, I would have been killed.

The pickup was wrecked. Even the roof was completely crushed down to head-height inside the car. Yet somehow I unbuckled the belt and crawled out, unhurt – or so I thought. I was terrified that the pickup would catch alight and I'd be trapped inside and burnt to death. I was therefore somewhat relieved to find that I was still in one piece. It wasn't until a few moments later, when I looked down and saw blood on my clothes, that I realised I'd suffered an injury. I didn't think it could be serious, as I was standing upright without experiencing any pain. But then I saw my right hand. The middle finger was covered in blood, but, worse still, it was totally mangled. I looked at the finger and was convinced I was going to lose it. And how many rugby players have you seen with a missing middle finger? My whole career seemed to hang in the balance at that moment.

I was taken to Malmesbury General Hospital, and the doctor on duty was not very positive. 'You've done serious damage to your finger. You could lose it,' he confirmed. Thanks, Doc, just what I needed to hear. I phoned our physio at Western Province, Bruce McLaughlin, and told him what had happened. 'Who is the best surgeon in the country,' I asked him, 'because I'm going to need him to save my career.' Bruce, who had worked tirelessly with me to help me recover from the anterior cruciate knee injury, could not believe what he was hearing.

He told me that a surgeon called Martin Wells was one of the best in the business, and he was based in Cape Town at the Panorama Medi-Clinic, a private hospital on the outskirts of the city. I was in theatre for four or five hours while they worked to save my finger. Eventually, very early the next morning, I awoke from the anaesthetic and looked at my hand. It was swathed in bandages, and I still had no idea whether I now had only four fingers, or a complete set. So I rang the buzzer, and a nurse came to my bed. I said simply, 'Do I still have my finger or not?'

She didn't know, and a pause that seemed to last a lifetime followed as she read the report on a pad attached to the foot of my bed. It was four o'clock in the morning, and there was deathly silence while I pondered the fact that my entire rugby career depended on what she would say next. After what seemed like ages, she looked up, her face not revealing any emotion, and said, 'Well, the report says you still have it.'

The next morning, the surgeon told me what a battle he'd had to save the finger. But if I thought my problems were over with that news, I was cruelly mistaken. I spent the next three months struggling to get the finger to work properly. I couldn't seem to catch a ball, and whenever I did, it hurt like hell. Basically, although they'd saved the finger, it was of little further use to me. I was receiving intensive physio, but it remained painful and inflexible. I was fit in terms of normal training, but I couldn't do anything that involved using my hand.

And that damaged finger was to cause me trouble for years to come …

I used to drive to the Panorama Medi-Clinic for physio, a forty-five-minute session aimed at obtaining more movement in the finger, but the treatment was extremely painful because the therapist would bend the finger repeatedly. I would be covered in sweat by the end of the treatment.

One day, as I was driving to Newlands from the hospital after a session, I noticed in the rear-view mirror a car sitting on my tail, something I don't like. I overtook the car in front of me, but the car behind did likewise, and again moved right up to my bumper. I looked down at my big, useless finger, which was sticking up awkwardly, and decided I could employ it very usefully in this situation. I stuck it in the air, making it plain what I thought of the man's driving.

Unfortunately I hadn't checked first to see who might be behind me. But I quickly caught sight of him when he overtook my car, swerved in front of it and tried to force me off the road. He was huge, big and bearded. And it was obvious from his behaviour that he wasn't pleased. He drove slower and slower, trying to get me to stop, but there was no way I was going to do that. He forced me onto the hard shoulder of the road, and at one stage he slowed down so much we were barely moving. It was crazy, dangerous driving on his part. I had quite a fast car, a VW Golf VR6, and thought I might be able to lose him, so I suddenly accelerated, overtook him and hared off. But his BMW quickly caught up, so I couldn't shake him off. The chase continued for over five minutes, but eventually it was obvious he was going out of his way. He pulled back, indicated he was turning off, but before doing so, drew a large, fat finger across his throat. The message was unmistakeable! And I can safely say now, years later, that it was the last time I ever showed anyone that finger while driving!

In the end, I decided I needed to play a rugby game to see how the finger would cope. So I played a match for Stellenbosch, against Oudtshoorn, in the club championships. Because I was so nervous that something would go wrong, it felt like I was playing in a test match! I was offered injections in the finger, but refused any, reasoning that I needed to know what pain levels would be involved and whether I could stand them. I didn't think I'd learn very much from playing with a deadened finger.

I made it through the game, although it was painful. But it was a giant step for me. After that match, Alan Solomons selected me for the Western Province squad, and I sat on the bench for the match against South Western District Eagles in the Currie Cup. I played thirty-five minutes of that game, and came through unscathed. I then played in the semi-final, the match against Griqualand West at Kimberley, which Western Province won 27-11. But there was to be no fairytale ending to a nightmare season for me: the Blue Bulls beat us 24-20 in the final at Loftus Versfeld in Pretoria.

On the basis of my recovery, I was selected for the Springbok squad to tour Britain and Ireland in November and December 1998 under Nick Mallett. I could hardly believe my luck, as I'd missed almost the entire season because of the injury.

I didn't play in any of the four tests on that tour – the 28-20 win over Wales at Cardiff, the 35-10 victory against Scotland at Murrayfield, the 27-13 win over Ireland in Dublin, or the 7-13 defeat by England at Twickenham. Incidentally, that defeat at Twickenham cost us a new world record of eighteen successive wins in test rugby. By then, everyone in the squad was exhausted. Most of the guys had played all year, and had to raise themselves for the eight-match tour of Britain and Ireland after their exertions during the long season. Twickenham proved to be one step too far.

I found just being with the Springboks on a major tour a fascinating experience. I saw up close how some of the best players in the world went about their business preparing for tough test matches. I could see how they trained, and how important relaxation and time away from rugby were to them. And I saw, too, how assiduously they prepared for every major match. Professionalism in rugby union may only have been going officially for just over three years in 1998, but the Springboks under Nick Mallett were a highly professional, intricately tuned outfit that did everything in preparation to ensure that they gave their optimum performance on match day. It was an eye-opening experience for me.

Since the operation on my finger, I had been unable to bend it properly, and I was always somewhat fearful of the possibility that it might just snap if it was hit or given a whack. In the end, I was lucky, because that never happened. I still have the finger to this day, but it's somewhat grotesque, swollen at the joints through arthritis, and it still hurts. When I started playing again, I found that it could be extremely painful if I ended up in a bad position. But somehow I managed to adapt when it came to carrying the ball. Essentially, I learnt to live with it.

Although 1998 had been another difficult year for me due to my injuries, I hoped that 1999 and the forthcoming World Cup, hosted by Wales, would be a whole lot better. But I was to be proven wrong. My hopes of participating in the World Cup late in the year were to end abruptly and cruelly in Dunedin against the All Blacks. That injury would put me out of rugby until the start of the 2000 season in South Africa.

But, before that, there was the pleasure of being involved in a fine Super 12 season with the Stormers. In 1998, we had finished the competition fourth from the bottom, ninth out of twelve teams. Unfortunately for South African rugby, two of the three teams below us that year were also South African – the Northern Bulls and the Golden Cats. The truth was, the South African sides were finding life hard in this highly competitive competition.

As a tournament, I found the Super 12 awesome. All the best players from southern hemisphere rugby were involved, and that led to a consistently high standard. Yet there are still improvements I would like to see in the competition. In my opinion, there should be promotion and relegation, so that you don't always play the same teams. I think playing the same sides has made the tournament a bit monotonous in recent years. It may also help if you had two pools of seven, instead of just one large pool of fourteen sides, as it will be in 2006 in the Super 14.

And what of the well-worn argument that a South African side will never win the Super 12 – or Super 14, for that matter – because of the travelling involved? Someone wrote recently that the Australian cricket team spent about 250 days away from home during one year, and they managed to keep winning. Why then, it was asked, do South African teams fare so badly when they travel?

But this missed the point. In South African rugby, there is a constant turnover of players within the teams. Australian cricketers can tour endlessly and keep winning because they are used to that lifestyle; they've been doing it for years. Players like Glenn McGrath and Shane Warne know no other way. But with the regular changes in the South African rugby teams competing in the Super 12, new players are always coming in. And they take a few seasons to get used to travelling for weeks on end across Australia and New Zealand. In no South African team are all of the players experienced travellers. That's the trouble.

And the fact is, it is very tough being away for a month or five weeks on a rugby trip. The weather is often dreadful down in New Zealand, especially on the South Island in wintertime. The time change is massive, the physical challenge you meet, likewise. And there is never enough time to adapt. Most people don't realise this, but just two or three hours' time change can take a massive amount out of you. Flying back and forth between New Zealand and Australia is extremely wearying.

Those factors are a significant problem, and the main reasons why, even today, in 2005, no South African side has ever won the Super 12 title. On most of the trips I made as a player to Australia and New Zealand for Super 12, we only ever won a maximum of two games out of four. And to be honest, we would be pretty happy with that. But to reach the semi-final and get a home game, and perhaps home advantage in the final, you will have to win the majority of your games. You can only afford to lose the odd match here or there. A ratio of 50 per cent on tour isn't good enough. It may get you into the semis, but not with home advantage, which is often so critical. I believe that a South African team has no chance of winning the Super 14 unless it plays a home semi-final and final.

Somehow, the competition organisers have to restructure the tournament so that the South African teams have parity with those of Australia and New Zealand. In other words, that we only have a maximum of two weeks on the road at any given time.

This problem goes to the core of a major issue I experienced throughout my playing career. South Africa has some of the best players in world rugby. But are we getting the best out of them in the way we structure our game? We have players good enough to win the Super 14, but if the rules and structures are so loaded against them, then it becomes largely impossible to achieve the ultimate success.

One other factor undermines the South African sides' prospects of being successful, and it is an aspect that sometimes makes me despair about South African rugby. South Africa is divided into regions, all of which are highly competitive with one another, with different cultures and backgrounds, and also different ways of thinking. Too often, the rivalry you would expect on the field becomes personal off the field as well. Some crowds at test grounds in South Africa boo certain Springbok players because they are from a different region, and that is really sad. That sort of attitude disappoints me.

These people have a very narrow view of South African rugby. They seem unable to put the regional differences behind them to support their national team. People say, 'Oh, there are ten players from Western Province in this team. I don't want to support them. I'm from Pretoria.' And the reverse is also true. This is probably the result of having been isolated from the rest of the world for so long. We turned inwards, caught up only in the interest of what was happening in our own backyard.

But isolation ended in 1992, and it is long past the time when we should have abandoned those old habits, and forged forward with a fresh, positive attitude. In those times of isolation, the only rugby competition for South Africans was between regional teams. Unfortunately, that became the be-all and end-all of our whole rugby existence. So much so that, even now, all these years later, some people still believe that if their team wins the Currie Cup they are virtually world champions.

Many people struggle to get past the fact that the Currie Cup is now nearly insignificant. It's nowhere near the biggest thing in the world any more; it's not even the biggest thing in South Africa. The Super 12 is ten times more important than the Currie Cup, and our complete focus should be on winning international competitions, not just bashing up one another to win local derbies. Five years ago, there was still some significance in the Currie Cup, but every year it has become less important. The focus now should be on getting people to think further than the Currie Cup, into the international arena.

In my view, all the Springboks should be pulled out of the Currie Cup. The competition should be for players not in the Springbok squad and the promising youngsters coming through. It would still create huge interest. But to force tired Springbok players, who may have just come home from Tri-Nations matches on tour in Australia and New Zealand, to throw themselves into the hurly-burly of such a domestic competition is misguided.

These players need to rest, so they can be fresher when it comes to what should be their No. 1 objective: winning more test matches. The players in the Springbok squad should play Super 12, Tri-Nations and the end-of-year tour. This is what the Australians do, and their record, up to 2004, speaks for itself, in all three competitions.

However, the best Super 12 team I saw during my playing career was the Auckland Blues, which won the tournament twice, in 1996 and 1997. In 1998, they lost to the Canterbury Crusaders by 13 points to 20 in the final in Auckland, but with their victories in the previous two years over the Sharks and the ACT Brumbies, they had demonstrated a complete dominance of the tournament. They had a team stacked full of expertise and talent. Up front, they had world-class forwards such as Sean Fitzpatrick, Craig Dowd, Olo Brown (what a front row!), Robin and Zinzan Brooke, Andrew Blowers, Mark Carter and Michael Jones.

Behind the scrum, there were exceptionally talented players like Jonah Lomu, Carlos Spencer, Junior Tonu'u, in his prime, Adrian Cashmore, Joeli Vidiri, Lee Stensness and Brian Lima. Graham Henry masterminded it all from the coaching bench. The quality of the players and the pace at which they played the game were exceptional. When you played them, they were innovative and clever, and very creative. They secured a lot of turnovers, from which they scored many tries. The Blues were also very good at the breakdown, never allowing your defence time to form properly. As a side, they were just magnificent – almost frightening to play against – and no South African team has ever come near that level of excellence in the competition.

Perhaps the closest was in 1999, when the Stormers had a fine team and a great year, losing to the Otago Highlanders in the semi-final. But we never dominated the tournament in the way Auckland had managed. That year was a missed opportunity for us, because, had we beaten the Highlanders, we would have faced the Canterbury Crusaders on our home ground at Newlands in the final. That would have been a massive occasion, but it was not to be.

Bob Skinstad was the Stormers captain at the beginning of the 1999 Super 12 campaign, but when he was injured, I took over as captain of both the Stormers and Western Province. The Stormers had some fine players that year, people like Cobus

Visagie, Robbie Kempson, Percy Montgomery, Robbie Fleck, Pieter Rossouw, Andy Marinos and Selborne Boome. Most of them had come through from the Under 21 group. Alan Solomons, whom I have always rated as a shrewd, clever coach and fine motivator, was in charge of our side. Even so, Otago nailed us on the day. Their team had been together longer and was a little more settled than ours. And yet they couldn't finish off the job on their own patch, losing 19-24 to the Crusaders in Dunedin.

Solomons was not a dictatorial type of coach. He may have had a specific way he wanted us to play, but he liked lots of player input too. I enjoyed his style of coaching. He wasn't big on discipline, as he relied on the players to be disciplined under their own personal code. As a team, we reacted positively to that, as we wanted to do well. There was a great understanding in the side, and we didn't want to let our mates down. We were disciplined when we needed to be, but we still partied hard after games.

But during that season an incident occurred that cast a shadow over all of us as players. It was the story of the Stormers' alleged strike threat. Early in the season, we had discussed bonus incentives with Rob Wagner, chief executive officer of Western Province Rugby Union. We agreed a match fee, and also win bonuses for home and away games. When it came to discussing bonus payments for the semi-finals and final, Rob's view was quite clear. 'We will cross that bridge if we get there,' was his attitude.

Frankly, I don't think he or the other Stormers' officials thought we would make the semi-finals. But when we did, I went into Rob's office at 9.30 on the Monday morning, well before the match the following Saturday, and said that we needed to discuss player incentives. I reminded him that we had left it open when we'd made the other agreements at the start of the season.

The players had decided to go for a percentage of the gate takings – 25 per cent, if I remember correctly – which would be spread among the squad. Rob listened, said that he would put our proposal to the board and get back to me by the Wednesday. I had no reason to feel concerned, as our discussion took place in a harmonious manner.

The plan that week was to train on Monday, Tuesday and Wednesday, have Thursday off, with the captain's run, as normal, on the Friday. We were preoccupied with training and preparations for the match in the first half of the week, and then we had the Thursday off to rest, so it wasn't until the Friday that I discussed the situation with the players' representative, Andy Marinos, our centre. Rob Wagner hadn't got back to me by Wednesday, as he'd promised.

Unfortunately, by then, word had leaked to a local Cape Town journalist who was close to the team that discussions were going on between the players and the board over bonus incentives. The reporter telephoned Andy Marinos and not me, even though I was the captain, and said: 'I hear you haven't yet sorted out your bonus payments.' Andy apparently told him fairly bluntly that if the matter wasn't sorted out within the next twenty-four hours, and if the players didn't get what they were asking, they might not play. He said he didn't care if the Union robbed a bank to get the money. It just came off the top of his head.

I didn't know that at the time, but when I did hear about it, I assumed it was just Andy kidding around. The players hadn't discussed any such thing and, as far as I knew, nothing could have been further from our minds. We had a home semi-final in the Super 12, with the chance of becoming the first South African team, at the time, to make the final. As soon as I heard about the call from the reporter, I telephoned Rob Wagner, but couldn't reach him. I left a message and went to bed.

When the newspaper came out the next morning, the words 'Strike threat' were blazed across the headlines. I usually woke up around 9.30 to 10 on the morning of a game, but was awoken at 7.30 that day by a telephone call from a friend.

'Are you guys going to play today or not?' he asked.

'What on earth do you mean?' I replied.

'Well, it says in the paper you're going to strike,' my friend said. I sat bolt upright in bed, knowing that there was trouble ahead.

We went to breakfast, and all the players were very surprised at the story, because no one even knew we hadn't confirmed our bonus incentive payments. Certainly, none of the players was aware that a strike was even a possibility, because it wasn't. We hadn't discussed one.

It transpired that everybody thought we had put a gun to the heads of the Stormers administrators, waiting until the day before the game to make our demands. But nothing could have been further from the truth.

Midway through the morning, I got a phone call from the founder and CEO of Pick 'n Pay, Raymond Ackerman. He said, 'Listen, what's the amount you're looking for?'

I think it was a sum of about R150 000, spread between thirty players, which was hardly going to make millionaires out of any of us. But he came up with the money, which, I have to say, Rob Wagner could have arranged earlier in the week to avoid all this nonsense.

I want to make it crystal clear: at no stage were we ever going to strike. It was just a silly throwaway line from Andy to a newspaper guy.

What was most disappointing of all was that we played the game, went 11-0 up, but were then blown away when Otago played brilliantly to seize the initiative. Tony Brown, their fly half, was absolutely magnificent. They took the game away from us, fair and square. But afterwards, inevitably, all the questions were along the lines of: 'Did the strike threat take your focus away from you?'

As captain, I was in a very difficult situation, because a lot of supporters thought we had betrayed them by holding Western

Province Rugby to ransom. But that was never the case. Rian Oberholzer, the CEO of SA Rugby at the time, was absolutely furious when he heard about what had happened. He called me in, and gave me an absolute mouthful. He told me that they wanted to go for Andy Marinos for what he had said. I also had to appear in front of a disciplinary committee, and in the end I had to pay R10 000 to a charity as punishment.

Did I think it was fair? Not at all. I'd never suggested a strike, because it hadn't even entered my mind. There was never the remotest possibility of such a thing. But, as captain, I was held responsible. In the end, I agreed to pay up just to make it all go away. What I couldn't do, even with money, was repair the damage that had been done to my name and reputation. Somehow, people seemed to believe that I had led calls for a strike, when nothing could have been further from the truth. But I had no way to defend myself, and my reputation suffered hugely because of the incident.

I am sure the South African Rugby Football Union (SARFU) acted because it felt the heat from public opinion. When pressure builds up, the rugby authorities feel they must do something. They make decisions based on pressure, not facts. It is a strange situation, but I saw it happen at first hand. Legally, there was no way in the world I should have been implicated or charged with anything in the affair. If anyone was to blame it was either Andy Marinos, for his careless choice of words to a media representative, or Rob Wagner, for not resolving the matter timeously. Yet I ended up being charged and fined. Absurd.

At least the disappointment of that near-miss in the 1999 Super 12 would be offset by the pleasure of making my test debut for the Springboks that season. But the serious injury I suffered against New Zealand in Dunedin later that year would dash all my hopes and dreams for the foreseeable future.

I don't know whether serious sports injuries make you stoical, but they certainly teach you patience. So, when I trotted out for my first game of the 2000 season, I had long since learnt to take the knock-backs, accept the reverses and bide my time for when I was fit again.

Philosophical? Well, I guess so. But I'll tell you this: I believe there is more to injuries than just luck, good or bad. For example, I believe there is a huge correlation between attack and defence and the amount of injuries sustained. If you play in a very defence-oriented team, I am convinced you pick up more injuries. You take constant hits if you are defending all the time, far more than if you play in an attack-oriented side. You get tired defending, lose your composure and are more likely to injure yourself when you go into contact. But when you don't have to absorb all those blows from opponents charging at you, you're much more likely to avoid injuries.

I can't say I have delved deeply into the statistics – for a start, I am no mathematician or statistician – but I have found this to be the case during my years in the game. Something else I noticed was the high number of injuries that occur in the last twenty or thirty minutes of the game. That, too, must have something to do with overall fatigue. Personally, I have had a lot of injuries in my career, and many of them were incurred while I was on defence. A coincidence? Some may say so, but I think not.

No sooner had I recovered from the serious knee injury that forced me to miss the 1999 World Cup than I picked up another, in the first months of 2000. The Stormers were playing a warm-up game against a Combined Western Province team, and thirty minutes into the game, I went in to tackle somebody. I got hit on the jaw, felt quite a lot of pain, but just tried to grit my teeth and carry on. I soon got another knock on the jaw, and this time I felt something move. A doctor came onto the field and said, 'You must come off, you've broken your jaw.'

The jaw was wired up for a month, and I was out for five or six weeks. I had to have all my food prepared in a blender and eat and drink everything through a straw. Many people lose as much as ten kilograms during such a period, but I managed to keep the weight loss down to one kilogram. Psychologically, that was one of the hardest injuries I ever had in my career. It was very painful initially, but being wired up makes it even worse. They reset the broken jaw and put a plate in to hold it together, wired through the gaps in your teeth. It's very painful when they remove the wires.

As a top-flight rugby player, you learn to accept injuries as an inevitable downside of life. It's like a businessman suffering from stress – it's part of the deal.

There was one highlight during the first few months of 2000, and that was when I met Nelson Mandela at the opening of parliament in February. At that time, I was in the Springbok side but was not yet permanent captain. I was invited to the occasion with Justine, my fiancée, and Bobby Skinstad and his girlfriend Debbie. After Mr Mandela's speech, his loyal assistant Zelda la Grange brought him over to meet the four of us at the reception. He had met Bob once before, but I remember I was in awe when I was introduced to him. We had our photo taken with him, and that picture still has pride of place in my home today.

The next time I met Madiba was when the Springbok squad was invited to his home in Houghton, Johannesburg. From there on, it seemed, we would meet him at least once a year. It was always an occasion I looked forward to with impatience and an enormous sense of pleasure.

Madiba really does love his rugby. Wearing that South African jersey for the 1995 World Cup final made him an indelible part of Springbok rugby. Ever since, players and public alike have seen him as a magic charm, someone who can really inspire the Springbok rugby team to great heights.

Later in 2000, he invited our little group of four, as well as Breyton Paulse and his girlfriend, to a private dinner with him at his home in Bishopscourt. There was no one in the world with whom I would rather have sat down to dinner. We arrived at around 6 p.m., and dinner was laid out informally in his kitchen. We were served a meal of traditional South African food, and Madiba enjoyed a glass of wine with his meal. We sat around the small table and talked, hearing about his life in prison. He told us how most of the white warders had treated him with the utmost respect. He is still in contact with one of them today. Even as a prisoner, the warders realised that he was a special man. You don't have to spend much time in Madiba's company to know just how special a human being he is.

Madiba told us that the one thing he had missed more than anything else during his years in prison was the presence of children. When you talk with him, you are constantly reminded of those values that mean the most in life: human relationships, the love of your family and friends, the gift of children and the pleasure they bring, and the delights of nature. On Robben Island, he had a very tiny stretch of soil on which he grew various shrubs and small plants. That small area inside the prison, where he could see things growing, gave Madiba tremendous pleasure, he told us.

The four of us sat almost dumbstruck, entranced by this humble man. Just to sit and listen to him, without other people to distract him, was an amazing experience. You don't want to spoil the moment by talking yourself. You want to hear him talk.

During the course of my years as a Springbok rugby player, I have been fortunate to meet many famous and distinguished people. But Nelson Mandela has stood head and shoulders above anyone else.

In 2000, I was captain of Western Province (and Gert Smal was coach) when we came from behind to beat Rudolf Straeuli's Natal Sharks 25-15 in the final in Durban to win the Currie Cup. We also beat them 29-24 in Cape Town the following year, to retain the Cup. Success gave us as a squad, and all our fans, huge satisfaction. But even we, the players, could see that the Currie Cup's importance had diminished compared to Super 12.

Before the 2000 final, we played a few mind games. In interviews before the match, a few of the WP players, including me, took the opportunity to say publicly that the Sharks were a dirty team, and they should control their players better. We were saying things like, 'Watch out, referee, they punch people off the ball,' et cetera. It was a bit below the belt, but it achieved its objective, because when we played the match, we noticed that the referee and his touch judges were watching the Sharks intently. That meant they couldn't play their normal physically intimidating game, and that undoubtedly inhibited them.

Mark Andrews, the Sharks captain, was especially upset with Breyton Paulse and me for some of our comments. He even took the highly unusual step of phoning me up in the days before the match and demanding to know what it was all about. When I heard him on the line complaining, I knew our policy had worked and that we were getting to them. The atmosphere for both finals was terrific, the excitement obvious. After the second victory in 2001, we said to ourselves, 'There's no reason why we shouldn't win five Currie Cups in a row here. We've got the players, so if we have the appetite, we can surely do it.' Our coach, Gert Smal, had achieved that back in the 1980s.

But consistency let us down. In 2002, we didn't perform as we should have, losing 13-50 to the Gauteng-based Lions in the semi-final, and then 2003 was World Cup year. It all sort of petered out.

The 2000 and 2001 successes were comeback wins and both were very satisfying. But the sweet taste of victory soured somewhat when we contemplated two years of comparative failure in the Super 12. In 2000, the Stormers weren't special, and then, in 2001, we started badly, losing 24-29 to the Cats in Cape Town. From then on, we were always on the back foot. We did win an away game on tour against the Hurricanes in Wellington, but lost disappointingly by a single point, 23-24, to the Otago Highlanders in Dunedin. Thereafter, we beat the Queensland Reds, Canterbury Crusaders, Waikato Chiefs and Northern Bulls, but lost to the ACT Brumbies, Auckland Blues and the Coastal Sharks. Won five, lost four. Points for consistency? Nil. We finally finished seventh on the log, with five wins and six defeats. It was another disappointing season in the competition, and we could not avoid the obvious conclusion: we just weren't good enough at that level.

Throughout my playing career, the fires of ambition and the desire to be a winner burnt strongly in me. I hated losing, loathed and perhaps even feared the thought of it. This was never something I wanted to acknowledge, still less accept or come to terms with. To me, if you go onto a sporting field even remotely thinking that you might lose, then you will. Someone once said, 'Show me a person who loses gracefully, and I'll show you a loser.' How true.

I wanted to win every single game I ever played. It was more than a vague ambition. It was a deep-seated, fierce desire to achieve and to win. I dared to reach for glory every time I went on a rugby field; it didn't matter whether it was Currie Cup, Super 12, a Springbok test or even a Barbarians fixture. I would entertain nothing less than victory.

I believe that to be successful as a top-class sportsman, you have to possess this attitude. Anything else will almost certainly mean that your eventual achievements will be that much less. I always tried to reach for the very top, to produce a top-notch personal performance in every single game I played. I wouldn't accept any lowering of my standards, although, inevitably, there were days when I fell short of the exalted levels I sought. When I did, I was bitterly disappointed in myself, and considered myself a failure. I wouldn't accept excuses from others, and I never accepted them in my own case, either.

But striving towards the highest levels of ambition can bring you crashing back to earth when things go wrong. And, as my international career as a Springbok began to gain momentum, I started to experience a bewildering mixture of highs and lows. At times, I felt sanity slipping from my grasp as international rugby football became the chief focus of my life.

6

Five Minutes of Madness: Twickenham 2002

The 23rd of November 2002 is a day I wish had never happened. Not for South African rugby, and not for myself.

They say that everyone would like to rewrite some of their history – airbrush out certain events or incidents in their lives they have regretted ever after. Twickenham 2002 is such a moment in my life. I have regretted the events that transpired during those eighty minutes of international rugby ever since.

For me, the long, painful road to Twickenham had begun early in the Currie Cup competition that year. I dislocated my right thumb playing for Western Province, and was in extreme discomfort. When the doctors examined me, they all agreed that an operation was necessary and that I should have it straight away. But that presented a major problem – I would miss the remainder of the domestic season.

It was therefore agreed that I would continue to play with the thumb strapped up, and see how it went. Those who have never dislocated a thumb will not know what such an injury feels like. My advice is, don't find out the hard way: it is very painful.

I tried to play on, but it soon became obvious I simply couldn't manage. It didn't matter how much medication or how many pain-killing shots I took to dull the pain – I just couldn't handle a ball properly and, when the drugs wore off, I was in agony. So I accepted the inevitable and had the operation.

The doctors told me I'd be out for six weeks, which would not only put me out for the rest of the season, but make my participation in the Springboks' end-of-year tour most unlikely. Rudolf Straeuli had been appointed Springbok coach on 1 March 2002, following the departure of Harry Viljoen, and had asked me to captain the team. When I saw him about my injury, we agreed that it wouldn't be a good idea to rush back, and that I should miss the tour. Nor was I alone – for a variety of reasons, several experienced South African players were not going to make the trip to Europe to play test matches against France, Scotland and England. I settled down to focus on healing my thumb, and forgot about the rest of 2002. My rugby year was over – now I had to focus on 2003, World Cup year. That would be at the forefront of my thoughts.

But things did not work out as expected. Rudi called me not that long after our original chat, and said that he felt he needed me on the tour, after all. He wanted to take a young Springbok squad, which would therefore lack experience. He was concerned that the balance was weighted too far in favour of youth, and he badly needed an experienced figure as captain, someone who had been around the block and knew what to expect. I had won twenty-eight caps since my debut in 1999 for South Africa, playing briefly under Nick Mallett and then Harry Viljoen, and had learnt a heck of a lot in that time. I understood exactly what it meant to wear the Springbok jersey. I knew what is was like to lie in bed the night before a test match and feel the nagging doubts about whether I could handle that level of rugby, as well as the physical intensity. I knew how it felt to sit in the dressing room an hour before the match, so nervous you felt physically sick. I'd been down that road, and by this time knew much better how to cope with the pressure.

I understood, too, the supporters' huge expectation of every player that pulls on the Springbok jersey. Springbok fans are the best in the world in my book, no arguing about that. They are passionate, deeply committed to the cause, and will urge you to achieve what you and they want more than anything else at that moment in time: victory. They are fanatical and wonderfully dedicated to the Boks. Time and again throughout my career, I had cause to thank them for their voluble support, for the huge inspiration they provided to keep me going. They helped me to fight through physical exhaustion and the pain of injuries. Somehow, when you heard those supporters continuing to shout for South Africa, you felt you would be prepared to run through fire for a victory. It was that powerful an emotion.

However, when you go away on tour, you lose home support. It is then that you find out what it is like to play in alien surroundings, on grounds where the opposition has all the support, and your every move is booed or jeered. In those circumstances, the emotional scenario is very different. You begin to feel like the whole world is closing in on you. Everyone is against you. Believe me, it is not an easy situation to handle.

But as Rudolf Straeuli began to gather together his squad for the three-match tour to Europe, he realised that he was desperately short on know-how. In particular, the absence of experienced players such as Bob Skinstad, Joost van der Westhuizen and Victor Matfield was an especially critical blow. They were all injured. This was at a time when France and England, two of the three countries we would meet on the short tour, were, in the words of one critic, 'a class apart' in northern hemisphere rugby. France had achieved the Grand Slam earlier that year in the Six Nations Championship, and England had finished runners-up, losing the crucial game 15-20 to France in Paris. It had been a titanic battle, and anyone who watched the match recognised that these two countries were likely to go far in the World Cup the next year.

Against such a backdrop, South Africa was assembling one of the most inexperienced squads it had ever taken on tour. No wonder Rudi Straeuli had his doubts. He called me up and asked me if there was a chance I might change my mind. 'I need you to come on this tour,' he said. 'We just haven't got enough experience in the team.' Unwisely – in hindsight – I agreed to hasten my recovery period and make myself available for the tour. I'd done four weeks' rehab work on the hand, and it seemed to be improving.

I said to Rudi that, in my view, winning or losing was not that important on this short tour. Of course we would set out hoping to win all three matches. But, I went on, our goal should be to discover just how many of the youngsters would really put their hands up to be counted. How many of them would show they had the mettle, the fire and resolve to handle playing international rugby and take the step up to the Rugby World Cup in 2003? One can only really find out about young players when they are in that sort of situation. Watching them in domestic competitions like the Currie Cup is one thing; seeing them perform in international rugby is something else entirely. By that time, Rudi would know the core of his World Cup squad for the following year, but, in a sense, that is always the easy part for any coach. It is much more difficult to add on the last ten names to the expected selection choices. I felt the end-of-season tour in 2002 should be used to test the younger guys, and whether they could make the step up to the World Cup squad. But Rudi disagreed.

'The public won't accept that,' he told me. 'We must say that we are going to the northern hemisphere to win all three games.'

Although Rudi was right, that kind of expectation would put great pressure on the team, bearing in mind that a lot of the touring party didn't have much experience. I could see problems ahead. Even though many of our top guys were injured and in desperate need of a rest before the World Cup, the public would never lower their expectations for the tour. Of course we always set out to try to win every game; show me a Springbok squad that hasn't done that. But South African supporters would never understand that this wasn't the first-choice squad, and that therefore there could be a couple of tough games along the way.

Although the South African rugby public understands the game better than almost anyone else in the world, perhaps with the exception of the New Zealanders, they are often prone to unrealistic expectations.

Rudi therefore said we were going to France, Scotland and

England to win. I thought to myself, the stakes have just been raised.

Although I understood why, I knew the extra pressure wouldn't help the youngsters to perform under such intense scrutiny.

But we flew to Paris and headed down to a beautiful French country estate somewhere near Marseille, at a place called Bandol. It was a hotel, golf course and wine estate, and one of the most beautiful places I have ever visited. Yet, during that week leading up to the test match, I hardly even noticed what a wonderful place it was or the facilities it offered. In the week prior to a test, a player just shuts everything extraneous out of his mind. This was particularly so for me in this situation, because I was the captain and I knew that the pressure was coming my way. I felt the huge responsibility keenly, especially when I looked at the young, inexperienced players around me. Bakkies Botha was there, Jean de Villiers too. But neither had yet played a single test match, although they would make their debuts that weekend against the French. Joe van Niekerk was in the team, and although he had fourteen caps, he'd only made his Springbok debut the previous year. And he had won seven of those caps coming on as a replacement. He certainly wasn't an experienced, grizzled test match veteran …

Fortunately, the front rowers James Dalton and Willie Meyer had been around the block quite a few times, but they were rare examples of experienced soldiers fighting this campaign. Mostly, we had a lot of youngsters who had never been bloodied, or who had played before but were only in their second or third season of international rugby.

As it turned out, Meyer got injured in the first half at Marseille and was replaced at half-time. That left us even shorter on experience, and, believe me, when you play any French international front row, you expect a battering. Wessel Roux took Meyer's place, and it proved to be a baptism of fire.

The French never really cut loose that day; they outscored us in terms of tries only by 2 to 1. But we conceded far too many penalties, an indictment of our indiscipline (Bakkies Botha was yellow-carded, just to add to our woes), our inexperience and the pressure we were under, and the French ran out easy winners by 30 to 10. It was a record victory margin for the French over South Africa, and it gave us a firm reality check. Suddenly we saw the strength of rugby in France at the time. We hung in there for most of the game, but, frankly, were lucky not to get annihilated. And our mood hardly improved afterwards when we heard that Meyer would have to return home because of his knee injury. We needed that news like a hole in the head. As we headed for Edinburgh to prepare to play Scotland at Murrayfield the following weekend, we resembled a battered, bashed team – that is what touring France is usually like.

Rudi Straeuli then made another cardinal error. It has always been my contention that, especially towards the end of a long season, when things get difficult, you should train less and less. It may sound misguided, and I know that many coaches would disagree with me. If your team loses, they will say, get them out on the field, train them hard and long, and iron out the faults.

But sometimes that is the worst thing you can do. The best coaches understand that they walk a thin dividing line between flogging weary players and allowing them to ease off, perhaps letting them off practice for a day or two. They will return refreshed and in a better frame of mind. I think that you should hammer guys on the training ground when they have won, to eradicate any suggestion of triumph or overconfidence, but ease off when they have lost – just give them a bit of TLC!

Rudi seemed calm when we spoke to him after that French match. But he revealed his true feelings during practice. Suddenly we could see how much pressure he was under. Serious calmness was called for in this situation, not panic. But Rudi was feeling the strain and he hammered us in training. And I know why.

After the match in Marseilles, Rian Oberholzer had come into the changing room and made it very clear that he was extremely pissed off. He berated some of the senior players for not taking responsibility. It was a bad mistake on his part – it was not the time or the occasion for that.

A player doesn't need to be told when he's had an ordinary game or when his team has failed to perform. And he certainly doesn't want to be told forcefully in front of all his mates. What is more, Oberholzer forgot that there were a lot of young players in the dressing room, many of them quite unused to international rugby. Climbing into the senior players in front of them was a serious error. I feared that it would put the younger players on the back foot mentally, forcing them deeper into their shell. As future events unfolded on the tour, I was proved right.

I was very upset when Oberholzer harangued the team, and I went straight to Straeuli and said, 'Get this bloke out of here.' That's how angry I was. But Rudi replied, 'He's the CEO, he has a right to be upset.'

I didn't accept that, but there was nothing I could do about it.

It didn't get any better at the after-match function. SARFU president Silas Nkanunu got up on stage, rambled on a bit and then asked the captain, 'Bob Skinstad', to come and say a few words. But Skinstad wasn't even on the tour. It hardly raised morale among a beaten squad.

When we arrived in Scotland, Straeuli sat us down and told us our defence had been disgraceful against France. We were going to have a tough tackling training session to try to sort it out. He gave one guy the ball, and two guys had to tackle him. Not very long into the training session, Marius Joubert, who had come on after just seven minutes for the injured Jean de Villiers at Marseille, went down with a shoulder injury, which ruled him out for the rest of the tour. It was another bad omen.

In short, we spent that training session bashing each other up. We trained with full-on contact and we absolutely destroyed each other. Had a spectator wandered onto the training ground and seen what was going on, he would have assumed it was a collection of bitter rivals all trying to smash each other to pieces. But in terms of commitment, I suppose you could say it was our best game of the tour. Unfortunately, it came on the training ground.

So, yes, it did get the guys fired up for the match. Scotland had been beaten three times in five matches in the Six Nations Championship earlier that year. Both England (29-3) and France (22-10) had thrashed them at Murrayfield, and they'd been wiped out 22-42 by Ireland in Dublin. The Scots were outscored by five tries to one in that game.

Scotland's worrying lack of playing resources meant that nine members of the side beaten in Dublin were again chosen for their game against us, eight months later. It was clearly a match we would have expected to win, and win comfortably.

But on the day of the game, we were absolutely diabolical. At one point, with Scotland ahead in the match, I remember looking at my teammates and thinking, 'How the hell are we going to win this game?'

A lot of the guys in the team should not have been there. The following statistical information should tell you everything you need to know about the South African side that started the match against Scotland that day: two of the side never played for South Africa again; seven of them would win just one more cap, against England a week later, and then never play for South Africa again; one player won two further caps, and another player three more, before never playing for South Africa again. In other words, within the course of just three more games, eleven of that side saw their international careers end. The brutal fact was that they just weren't good enough. They should not have been wearing the Springbok jersey.

We lost 6-21 to Scotland on a day of foul weather – and also thanks to a second-rate refereeing performance by Nigel Williams of Wales. He awarded a very doubtful try to Scotland, which he never referred to the TMO (television match official). Later that evening, at the official dinner, I happened to be signing something at his table, and someone came up to him and asked, 'How did you award that try?' And he basically admitted that he had just given it and hadn't bothered to refer it upstairs. Suddenly, he looked up and saw me standing there, and he was as embarrassed as hell.

But not even Mr Williams's dubious decisions could mask the fact that too many of our team just weren't up to the task. It concerned me greatly that our second-string players looked so weak. The strength of Springbok rugby? It simply didn't exist at the time.

From Scotland, we flew down to London for what I feared was going to be the toughest match of the tour. And it was going to be even tougher, because the team was plainly lacking confidence. Although there was some brave fighting talk, there was no fire-power. What was more, we had to choose eleven of the same players to go out and face England. We just didn't have reserves of sufficient calibre to make major changes.

Whenever I represented the Springboks, I set out to give absolutely everything I had to try to help the side win. I never gave anything less than 100 per cent in every single game. But in the week before the match against England at Twickenham, I didn't think that we could win. I just couldn't see how we could possibly turn things around so dramatically. As I've said, I didn't feel we had the players for the job anyway, as France and Scotland had shown us. But now came the powerful England side, a team everyone touted as one of the main contenders for the World Cup in Australia in 2003.

I understood the enormity of the task ahead of us. In the event, England fielded twelve of the side that would go on to beat Australia to win the World Cup in Sydney twelve months later. The only changes from the side that played us to the one that lifted the Rugby World Cup were Trevor Woodman for Jason

Leonard in the front row, Lawrence Dallaglio for Lewis Moody in the back row, and Josh Lewsey for Phil Christophers in the back line. Otherwise, we were in effect playing the future world champions. And we had to do it with a side that we all knew just wasn't good enough – not just to meet a team as powerful as England, but to play international rugby.

I hoped against hope that England, knowing we'd lost twice already on the tour, might underestimate us. If they took their eyes off the ball, as it were, we might in those circumstances get quite close to them.

We trained hard again during the week, paying even more attention to our defence. We had a few good defenders, players like Robbie Fleck, Breyton Paulse, AJ Venter and Joe van Niekerk. And, in the event, AJ had a big game at Twickenham on the day.

England had won the previous three matches between our two countries at Twickenham, yet, in the first fifteen minutes, it was a tightly fought contest. But after twenty-three minutes, with England leading 8-0, New Zealand referee Paddy O'Brien waved the red card at our lock Jannes Labuschagne for a late tackle on England fly half Jonny Wilkinson. At the time, even our critics suggested it was a harsh punishment for the offence. However, only moments before, O'Brien had given a general warning to both teams to cut out the niggling that had been there from the start.

I have to say that I always had huge respect for Paddy O'Brien during his time as an international referee. I also enjoyed him as a person, as he wasn't one of those big-headed referees you come across in the game. Paddy was always humble – a fantastic, nice guy. But, having said that, I do think he made a big mistake to give a red card to Jannes. There may have been some malicious intent in Jannes's tackle, but it did not warrant a red card. A yellow one, fine, but not red. Jannes's challenge was late, but I've seen far worse tackles go unpunished.

Now that we're on the subject, I want to stand up and say

With Harry Viljoen at a training session in Windsor, England, November 2000

With 'Sir William' (Willie) Meyer, after practice, Windsor, England

The test against England at Twickenham on 2 December 2000

Celebrating one of my few tries for the Stormers, against the Chiefs, with Bobby Skinstad, April 2001

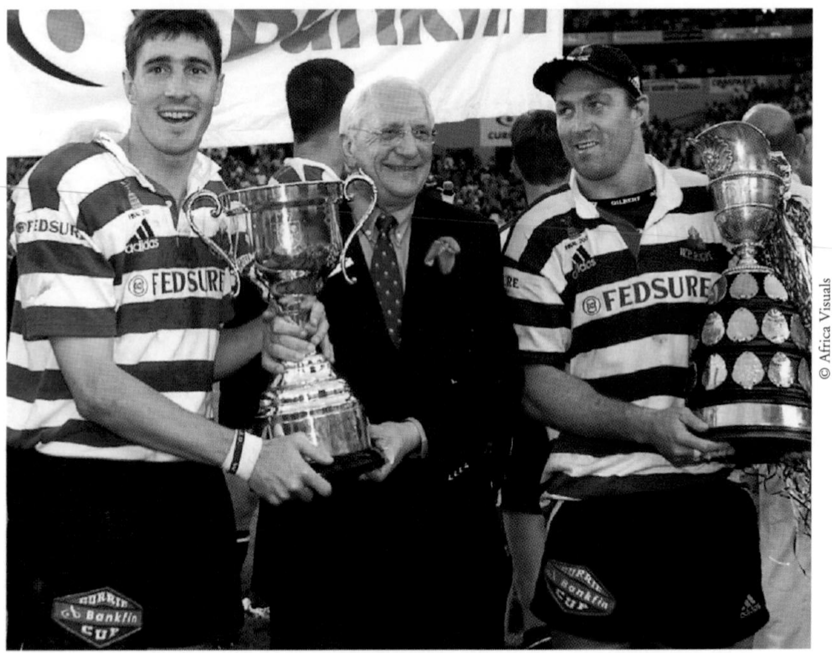

Winning the Currie Cup against the Sharks for the second consecutive year, this time at Newlands, on 27 October 2001. Pieter Rossouw and Koos Basson are next to me

Tackling Jonah Lomu. Stormers versus Hurricanes, March 2002

Leaving the field injured in the same game

After a training session

Twickenham, 23 November 2002.
Abel, our mascot, accompanied us on the tour

Five minutes of madness: one of the many notorious moments in the England–South Africa game. Martin Johnson has his arm around my neck

Playing the game

Scoring a try against the Sharks in the Super 12, February 2003

Beating the Waratahs at Aussie Stadium, Sydney, March 2003. I have my legs wrapped around Pierre Uys

With George Gregan, captain of the ACT Brumbies, at Canberra Stadium, March 2003. We didn't win that one

Congratulating Louis Koen on scoring in the last minutes of the game against Argentina, June 2003

Face-off with my 'fellow countryman', George Gregan, during a Tri-Nations match at Newlands, 12 July 2003

Holding the Mandela Challenge Plate after our victory over Australia at Newlands

Taking it personally: losing 16-52 to New Zealand at Loftus Versfeld, Pretoria, 19 July 2003

Shouting encouragement to the team

A perk of the job: meeting two of the Corr sisters during the 46664 concert in Cape Town in 2003

definitively that I personally got it horribly wrong at Twickenham that day. Over two years later, Paddy O'Brien wrote in a South African newspaper that, when he saw a tape of the game some time afterwards, he was appalled at what had gone on behind his back. 'I should have sent off five of them,' was his comment.

And I have to say that he was right. And that I should have been one of those sent off.

To this day, I still struggle to understand what went on inside my mind that day at Twickenham. When people ask me to describe my feelings and emotions during the game, I think back and recall all sorts of things. What happened came from a combination of spirit and the heightened sense of competition. Then there was the obvious desire not to lose, and refusing to accept defeat graciously. And there was the anger and resentment I felt towards England's arrogance. After all, we had lost in Marseille and Edinburgh and nothing like this had happened there. But then we hadn't perceived our opponents to be arrogant, as if they were trying to rub our noses in defeat. France and Scotland had enjoyed beating us, as one would expect. But they did not exhibit the sneering superiority of the England team as they put us to the sword at Twickenham.

In fact, England was the team I disliked playing against the most, for they were always full of it. I didn't particularly dislike playing any other team, like New Zealand, Australia or Ireland. But England was different. Because of their supercilious attitude, they were never good opponents.

As we played Australia and New Zealand more often, we came to know the players better. We would go into their changing rooms after matches, and have a beer and chat with them at the after-match functions. We became friends with several of their players. But I never felt that way about England. Until the World Cup in 2003, when I talked to guys like Martin Johnson and Phil Vickery after a game, I'd never had a beer or spoken with any of their players socially. At least the 2003 World Cup pool match between South Africa and England was played in a much better spirit, but before that, England, and especially players like Matt Dawson, Austin Healey and Ben Cohen, were very condescending. And so was the attitude I encountered from one of their England internationals when I later joined the English club Northampton.

As youngsters in South Africa, we were always taught to be good losers, to be gracious to our opponents when we lost, no matter how painful the defeat. But when it came to playing England, not many of their players were good winners either. Quite a few of them really wanted to rub it in when they were beating you. And that just helped to infuriate us at Twickenham.

Make no mistake, I'm not trying to make excuses for my actions in that match. I accept my full share of the blame, as well as responsibility for what the Springboks did on the field that day.

I had lost at Twickenham before, and knew what it was like. But then Paddy O'Brien stunned everyone on the field and the crowd of 70 000 spectators by red-carding Jannes Labuschagne. From then on, we were on the back foot. Playing with only seven men against their forward pack was a nightmare. That imbalance in strength, combined with England's attitude, motivated me to be as dirty as I could for the rest of the game. I knew that we were going to lose, but I made up my mind to take a few people down with me.

I committed some appalling fouls, hitting people in possession and smashing others off the ball. Of course, not only was it dangerous play, but also stupid. It only raised England's ire to such an extent that they thrashed us 53-3, the worst beating a Springbok side has ever suffered. And you can imagine how I felt as the team's captain. You can choose whichever words you wish: humiliation, hurt, pain, anger, resentment, fury; all of them applied to my state of mind that afternoon as we trudged off Twickenham.

When I sat down in the dressing room after the final whistle, I just cried my eyes out. I was mentally shattered and in great physical pain. I had bashed my body so badly that I was in agony. I honestly believe that I took two years off my rugby career in that game. My body was destroyed.

I cried through sheer pain and frustration. We'd had a terrible tour, lost all three games and been caught up in this total humiliation at the end of it. It was hard to take.

Of course, the British media – especially the tabloids, whose appetite for scandal is as intense as Dracula's for blood – had a field day. There was a photograph of me elbowing Martin Johnson in the face. However, the picture didn't show what had happened moments earlier: Johnson strangling me, so much so that I thought I was going to lose consciousness. I was literally fighting for breath, and, in order to break his grip, I swung an elbow at his face. It was done just to try to get him off me, as an act of survival. But of course people went berserk about that incident, not wanting to hear what had led directly to it.

Twelve months later, when we got to the World Cup in Australia, I would again be surrounded by the British media, about a remark I had made to a South African journalist – one I had thought would be off the record. In the event, it found its way into the press. I had called Johnson one of the dirtiest players in the world, and of course the British media latched onto my statement like pit bull terriers as soon as the Springbok squad arrived for the World Cup.

During the Twickenham match, I flew into rucks boots or head first. I felt no concern for my own safety or for the safety of others. I suppose you could say the red mist had descended; I really lost it badly. The worse thing I did was to try to knock Matt Dawson out with a flying headbutt. I considered him one of the most arrogant guys in the team. But I admit I was concerned when I heard that Dawson had suffered a neck injury, which at one stage was thought to be so serious that it might put an end to his career. It didn't, but I wasn't proud of my actions.

To compound matters, after the match our coach Rudolf Straeuli was questioned by British journalists about our rough-house antics. Straeuli bristled at the suggestions and said, 'We have two players concussed and one with a dislocated shoulder. Do you think we concussed ourselves?'

Unfortunately, Rudi had not been warned that Sky Television had footage showing me throwing a punch at an opponent, missing, and my fist connecting with the face of André Pretorius, our fly half. I felt extremely embarrassed afterwards, as I knew the blow with which I had inadvertently felled André would not only make me look stupid, but would backfire on Straeuli for what he said at the press conference.

At this point, I have to state emphatically that Rudolf Straeuli did not condone dirty play or encourage us to bend the rules.

I was very lucky to get away with the incidents in which I was involved. I should have been sent off. And I was also lucky that, afterwards, the only player cited by the match referee was Werner Greeff, our fullback, for a dangerous, head-high tackle on Phil Christophers, which cost us a penalty try and brought Werner a charge of foul play.

Twickenham 2002 was a total disaster for all South Africans, but especially for me. It has taken me years to get over that one game. Indeed, it is only recently that I have begun to deal with it. People kept reminding me about the match during my time in England with Northampton, and it was as though I would never escape it. Today, when I look back, I certainly wouldn't argue with O'Brien's comment that five of us should have gone off.

And yet, in a sense – and this might sound bizarre – I would rather do what I did than chuck the towel in, as some of the other Springbok players did. I'm not going to name them, for they know who they are. Suffice to say, I'd rather be guilty of overreaction than capitulation. I could never have lived with myself had I done that.

I was very disappointed in those players who gave up. I knew a lot of them would never play for South Africa again. They never stood with me on the field, or afterwards when I was in a deep state of mental anguish and physical pain. I felt I was in a minority, and that intensified the agony.

So did the score: 3-53 is an absolute thrashing, and I still don't think we deserved that. It added insult to injury.

It was only comparatively recently that I found out about Rian Oberholzer's behind-the-scenes influence on the IRB, which wanted to have a look at the video evidence and bring me before a disciplinary hearing. It was Corné Krige's five minutes of madness, and it would have provided damning evidence against me. When one person is involved in five or six bad incidents, like I was, it does look disgusting.

But apparently Rian worked extremely hard behind closed doors to persuade the IRB not to go ahead with their plan. He convinced them not to put me through it, for he knew I would probably be banned for a very long time.

If they had banned me for long enough to rule me out of the World Cup the following year, I would have given up rugby there and then. I was at such a low ebb that nothing would have persuaded me to stay in the game and come back ever again.

The full extent of what had happened at Twickenham remains a mystery to a lot of South Africans, because the video footage was never shown in its entirety on South African television. I'd be the first to say that I think it should have been. I don't advocate banning such a film simply to protect me or anyone else. In my view, the South African public should have been shown that footage.

There is something else I'd like to set the record straight about concerning England. Martin Johnson was definitely *not* one of the arrogant members of the England side. I will still say that he was a dirty player. Follow him on camera in any game he played, slow the action down and watch some of the things he got up to. But, as a rugby player, you have to live on the edge, especially when you play in the tight five and the loose forwards. I'm not saying you should step over the edge often, but you just have to be right up there in the aggression and physical stakes. Part of the game, especially at test match level, is about physical intimidation and domination – that is what makes rugby unique. It is very much part of the game. Johnson was extremely tough and sometimes violent, and I had personal experience of that. But he was never arrogant.

Today, as I cast my mind back on that match from the altogether calmer world of sporting retirement, I struggle to believe that it was really me who'd been involved. I have a wife and child, friends and family. I live a decent, ordinary life; I am not a hit man, an assassin. But I regret that day more than any other in my entire rugby career.

I let down the Springbok team and its emblem and image, the South African people, myself. Even today, I am still deeply embarrassed whenever I see any of that footage on television. But my philosophy in life has always been: If you are in the wrong, front up, accept the criticism, take it on the chin, and then move on. Do not complain if you are responsible for your own misfortunes – which I was.

Twickenham 2002 has hung over my head ever since.

The truth is, I should never have gone on that tour, and now I will always regret the fact that I did. Had I not done so, I would have saved myself an enormous amount of trouble in subsequent years. But things always happen for a reason, even if we are not aware of it at the time.

And now, for the very last time, please accept my full and final apology. From the moment this book is published, I will consider the Twickenham incident to be finally consigned to the past.

7
War Games: Kamp Staaldraad

Four days in the bush at a camp: I could think of few things I'd rather do. I had been out camping in the bush for most of my life. But events at the camps I had known were to bear no relation whatsoever to those that happened at the notorious Kamp Staaldraad, or 'Camp Barbed Wire'.

The time was drawing nearer for the World Cup squad to be announced, and Straeuli had picked forty-five players to join him for three weeks of intense physical training and tactical preparation at the High Performance Centre at the University of Pretoria. Only thirty of those would eventually be selected for the World Cup. It turned out to be a difficult time for the players, as the pressure was on to perform, and the Geo Cronjé/Quinton Davids incident, which I will discuss in more detail in Chapter 9, only exacerbated the tensions already in the group. After the announcement of the final World Cup squad, we were told that we would be leaving the city to attend a camp in the country, presumably not only to test our endurance, but also to avoid the fallout from the alleged racial incident.

Rudi Straeuli had called in Joost van der Westhuizen, John Smit and myself, and told us we were going on a military-style camp to get away from the press, and to allow the players time to bond. Although he did not reveal any details of what we could expect at the camp, he did warn us that it would be a particularly gruelling experience.

My initial reaction was positive. I had experienced something similar with Alan Solomons during his period as Stormers coach in 1999, and it had been absolutely fantastic. We had gone to the town of Saldanha on the West Coast, and we participated in brilliant activities. We swam in the sea at midnight, went through an obstacle course and ran for miles. We performed a lot of physical and mental tasks, but the work had been offset with fun things like waterskiing and diving for crayfish. That camp had been about enjoyment, uplifting the players and team building. We had a great time, and when we left, we felt on top of the world.

Kamp Staaldraad was to be very different, a world away from those pleasures. Its core intent was to break us down mentally and physically. Then, presumably, we were to be rebuilt into a strong, close-knit unit.

There is definitely a place for thoroughly testing the fitness of professional sportsmen in the modern game. At around the same time as we were heading for Kamp Staaldraad, England were on an exercise with the British Army's renowned Royal Marines at their Exmouth base on the Devon coast. The players had to do things like carry logs together across mud flats, and go on night marches. It fully examined just how fit the English players were, and also helped their team bonding.

In theory, it is true that individuals subjected to adversity together bond more quickly and become closer than would otherwise have been the case. They find solace and comfort in the presence of others, sometimes people with whom, under normal circumstances, they would have had nothing in common. Put them in a crisis situation and they draw together. That is established theory in the world of psychology.

I was not surprised at the timing of Kamp Staaldraad. The media had been hounding us, criticising us intensely in the light of the alleged racist incident that had occurred during the Bok training camp. There was tremendous fallout from that, and Straeuli thought it essential that we get away from the furore and refocus on the task before us: winning the World Cup. To that effect, he said that a camp had been arranged.

The South African squad headed out from Pretoria to the camp on a Saturday evening, on 30 August 2003. The World Cup was by then just six weeks away.

With hindsight, it is easy to see that we should just have blocked out the media criticism and avoided the press. It would not have been impossible. But Rudi Straeuli wanted to try to control and manipulate the press. He wanted to determine what they wrote and didn't write, and, in this case, events were out of his control.

There was a word of warning about what might lie ahead of us at the camp. Joost said he had attended a camp with the Blue Bulls, and, in his view, if this camp was anything like it, it would be very tough, but ultimately good for the players. Joost, John and I had been given no particular details about the camp by Straeuli. We didn't know its location, or how long it would go on for.

The immediate build-up to this trip had been a traumatic time for us all. The World Cup squad was to be announced during a big ceremony, but Rudi nearly refused to let the squad participate because of the inquiry into the Geo Cronjé/Quinton Davids incident. Basically, although it was found that were no grounds to find Cronjé guilty of racist conduct, the investigation would stay open. Pandemonium broke loose. Straeuli said that he would not take the players to the ceremony unless the investigation was closed. But the sponsors were involved and the public would also attend the event, and in the end Straeuli relented, and we did what we had to do. We showed our faces. We had a squad photograph taken and sang the national anthem. I remember being very emotional: it had been a tough week for all of us. I thought to myself, 'At least we can start focusing on the World Cup, which is what we are all here for anyway.'

Eventually, after signing hundreds of autographs, we boarded the team bus and headed back to the Tuks High Performance Centre in Pretoria. On the way, our manager said that everybody had to meet in the team room as soon as we got there.

The first surprise was that Adriaan Heijns was running the meeting. Heijns was the Springboks' security consultant, a former

South African Police Task Force commander who now had his own security company. During the 1995 World Cup, it was his job to look after security at the stadiums. By all accounts, Heijns's company had done a brilliant job.

Now Heijns told us that we were going on a camp, and listed what we had to wear: rugby shorts, a T-shirt, a pair of socks and shoes. We should also bring a spare pair of socks and shoes, tracksuit pants and a toothbrush. That was all we would be allowed to take with us. We would be issued with rugby jerseys on arrival.

We set off and drove for about two hours. Eventually, the bus stopped on a dirt road, and we were told to get off. A truck was parked on the side of the road. We were lined up, and Heijns said, 'Welcome to Kamp Staaldraad.'

We were told that for the next three days, Heijns and two of his men would have total control of us. Rudi would have no influence whatsoever; he would simply be an onlooker. Heijns told us we would be put through physical and mental tests, to see who could make it and who couldn't. He said, 'If you can make it, you can go to the World Cup.'

But the World Cup squad had just been announced! The names were, at that moment, winging their way around the world on the news wires. Yet now it was being implied that we were *on trial* to go to the World Cup. Our participation was apparently not yet confirmed. Adriaan Heijns was telling the South African rugby squad, which had just been announced to represent the country at the World Cup, that there were doubts as to their participation in the tournament. Perhaps it could only happen in South Africa.

Heijns's final words to the squad bore an even more chilling message. He said that it would be most unwise for anyone to revolt against them. 'I wouldn't recommend it, because we will be carrying firearms,' he said. He wasn't joking, either.

I suppose, looking back, that was the first moment I had an

indication of what we'd been pushed into. The psychological aspect to modern-day, professional sport is a widely discussed topic that has been explored in all manner of ways. Some of the results of those discussions have undoubtedly been beneficial to the development of sportspeople's abilities. But the problem is, sometimes ideas run away with people. They lose the plot and end up trying the most ludicrous, far-fetched ideas that clearly have no relevance whatsoever to a sports team.

What was the reaction of most of the guys? Some of them were laughing, others farted to offset Heijns's ominous warning, and to take the mickey out of him. That led to a bout of collective giggling. But Heijns did not have a smile on his face. You could tell he was back in an environment he knew well, and in that place people did not joke or fool around. His response was to order us to do a set of push-ups, clearly a punishment intended to remind us of his background in the Special Forces. The players regarded most of the Special Forces guys as a different breed, a view that would be more than justified during the next seventy-two hours.

When we'd finished the push-ups, Heijns ordered us to strip. All our clothes had to be removed and piled up beside us. He and his men searched every item of clothing to see if we were hiding anything, but they found nothing. We stood there, stark naked, looking bemused as they searched our pants, as though we were a group of terrorists they'd just hauled in. Then we were each handed a red rugby jersey with a number on it. From that moment, we were just a number.

When that little scene had been enacted, Heijns said, 'Right, you have one minute to get dressed and get onto the truck.' Then we set off into the bush, the truck bumping over the rough terrain, throwing us around. We sat there wondering what the hell we were in for. They had taken our watches, so we didn't know what time it was. But it was dark by now.

We came to a clearing, the truck stopped and we were ordered off. We were split into pairs and told to walk deeper into the bush, where we would find a log. There were fifteen logs for the thirty guys. Our task was to lift these logs onto our shoulders and march down the road. It was a tough job, because the logs were massive. We had to change shoulders after a while because they were so heavy. But if you put the log down or dropped it, you had to go back to where you had started and do it all over again. And the only way to get the log back to the original starting place was to carry it. In other words, one slip and you were punished.

We must have walked for over an hour with the logs on our shoulders, although it was impossible to tell exactly without watches. What we did know was that we were exhausted. When we finally reached the clearing, the guards (it's an appropriate word, as we were being guarded: they had in effect told us that any resistance was useless) said we could put the logs down. 'Put', mind you, not drop. One of the guys dropped his log and was punished. Because he had 'messed up', we all had to undergo the same punishment. We had to leopard-crawl into a black, burnt field on our stomachs. I think it was then that I fully realised this was going to get serious.

Our next task was to split into three teams of ten each, and we were sent off to another place a few hundred metres away. There we found three massive tractor tyres, each with a chain attached. The tyres were different sizes, but all were pretty big and extremely heavy. Between the ten of us, we were ordered to pick them up and start marching. This was a nightmare to do, because you couldn't balance the tyres and chains properly. All we could do was march a short distance. We were told that if we couldn't go further, we were to put them down and then pick them up and start again. This was a neat little twist, because picking them up in the first place was the worst part.

Somehow, we managed to lift these unbelievably heavy objects and march down the track. We went on for what seemed ages, before finally collapsing. Then they gave us water. It is hard to calculate exactly how long these exercises went on for, but they lasted all night, because they told us when the sun came up we would be allowed to sit on the tyres and rest. It was quite cold during the night, for it was still winter. And all we had on was a thin shirt and shorts.

The exertion was so intense that as soon as the sun appeared and the guys collapsed in a heap, they fell asleep straight away. But the rest period was cruelly short.

They had us ready to go again in no time, and we had to embark on a forced march and a jog lasting hours. We must have covered many kilometres. We also had to sing the whole time, just like US marines or soldiers in a Hollywood movie. The people who had put these exercises together obviously watched that kind of movie for inspiration. But their version had a nasty twist. If you stopped singing, you were punished either by having to do a series of push-ups or by crawling on your stomach through the fields and scrub. And if you were out of sync when you marched – left, right, left, right – everybody was stopped and punished.

Basically, they just wanted to dish out punishment, and they came up with a long list of petty mistakes to enable them to do so. We were being stopped almost the whole time for punishments.

What did I think? Basically, I felt the whole thing was rubbish, but I didn't know what might happen next. Perhaps there would be a few beers and a braai at the end of it, around normal breakfast time. I couldn't have been more wrong. I had totally underestimated these guys.

They said that when we'd done more marching and jogging, plus sung as much as the birds at dawn, we could sleep. And then we'd get about half an hour. Of course it was impossible to be exact, but I have a fair idea of what thirty minutes is, and we didn't even have enough time to fall asleep before they called us again.

The next 'activity' – 'trick' would be a better word – involved rugby balls and the lake. At least with the rugby balls, we were reminded that we actually were rugby players. We made the connection! We were marched down to the lake, each given a ball, stripped and told that we had to pump the balls up in the water, half-air, half-water. The water was absolutely freezing, like ice. The problem was, there were only two or three pumps.

I would estimate that we were in the lake for at least two hours. Of course, we were struggling to pump the balls up, as they knew we would. Some of the balls would have lots of water in them and hardly any air, and trying to hold them properly in the water and apply the pump with frozen fingers and a body that was freezing was next to impossible. Which, I imagine, was the intended effect.

Eventually I was so cold, I was getting massive cramps in my body, and the guys told me my lips were turning blue. I believed them, because theirs were too.

I moved around among some of the guys and said, 'Look, let's get out of the water.' I spoke to Breyton Paulse, Louis Koen, Stefan Terblanche and a few others. They said, 'If you go out, we go.'

By now it was late morning, perhaps even early afternoon. We had not eaten a thing for almost twenty-four hours. But our guards, to emphasise their sadistic tendencies, had lit a fire and had a braai going. We watched as they cracked open a few beers, and the smell of the boerewors wafted down towards us in the freezing water. But the food and beers were just for them, of course.

I didn't think of it at the time, but I thought afterwards, 'Gee, if this is what you have to go through to play in a Rugby World Cup, I'm glad I never got anywhere near the Olympics. Now *that* would be tough.'

Back in the lake, we'd been told the water must come up to our necks. But I whispered to a few of the guys that I was going to walk out of there. I'd had enough of the shit. I told them I expected them to follow. Players like Louis Koen were only too keen to join me; they were really struggling to survive the intense cold.

I started wading out of the water, and every player, except for one, followed. Faan Rautenbach, our prop forward, stayed behind. He had sufficient body fat to survive far longer than the rest of us, but I was bitterly disappointed that he failed to follow his teammates. I felt he'd let the rest of us down. However, he and I later had a good talk and managed to clear up the matter.

The guards were so busy filling their stomachs with food and talking among themselves, they didn't realise what was happening until most of us were out of the water. Once they realised what was going on, they started screaming at us: 'Did we tell you to get out of the water? What the hell are you doing?'

I started to say that this was totally unacceptable, that some of us were struggling to survive the cold. And the next moment I heard gunshots. They were aiming their guns at the lake, and the bullets were tearing into the water on either side of us. 'Get back in there!' they shouted. Frankly, without much argument, we went back in.

I have asked myself a thousand times since whether it was a mistake to go back into the water. At the time I told myself no, because they would have got us back in there somehow. To walk out was the right thing to do, but my strategy was not sufficiently well thought through to cover all eventualities. That wasn't surprising, as I was so cold I could hardly think straight. When your body is freezing, your mental capacity slows down significantly.

Today, I know what I should have done. I should have kept on walking out of the water, leading those players who wanted to follow their captain. I should have walked right out of that crazy lunatic asylum of a camp. But I knew that I would have needed the support of the senior players. I believe most of them would have backed me, but I was worried about Joost. He enjoyed that sort of stuff and had gone through it before – or something like it. And before the camp had even started, he'd mentioned that those of us who didn't complete it might be thrown out of the squad. I therefore doubted that he would have supported me.

And, to be honest, I was worried about the threat of being dropped from the World Cup squad. I had never been to a World Cup, and I sensed that 2007 would be just too far over the horizon for me to consider. The 2003 tournament was likely to be the only one in which I would be able to participate. Did I want to throw that away in a moment of ill temper? Was I certain that most of the squad would follow my lead?

Had I been, I would have kept on walking. But to my eternal regret, I went back into the ice-cold water. It is no use trying to cast blame on others for my actions. I realise now that, as the captain, I was the one who should have taken control of the situation. I should have said: 'That's it, we are not going back into the water. You can do what you like.' I don't think they would have shot twenty or so Springbok rugby players on the spot, nor would a whole lot of us been ejected from the World Cup squad. Think of the headlines and the implications for Rudolf Straeuli and the bosses at SA Rugby when *that* story came out! It was bad enough when the events at Kamp Staaldraad eventually reached the media. Both the coach and chief executive of SA Rugby lost their jobs, chiefly as a result of what went on at the camp.

But hindsight makes experts of us all. When I look back now, I am humiliated and angry at what happened. And I suppose the greatest humiliation was being forced to undress and stand around naked. That might sound odd when it is common knowledge that rugby players undress in front of one another every week when they are about to play a match. But this was different. It was a contrived, wholly artificial situation in an atmosphere permeated with physical threats.

Another humiliation followed when we got back into the water. My body temperature quickly plummeted again. The only way I could manage to retain any body heat was to be hugged in the water by Rautenbach. I found that both humiliating and degrading. Which is presumably what those who had planned this wanted us to feel.

Cold is my weakness. Having been born in Zambia and lived in Cape Town, I never grew accustomed to really cold weather. The first time I encountered anything like it on a long-term basis was when I joined the English Premiership club Northampton and lived through an English winter. When I returned to Cape Town at the end of my stint, in time for the Cape winter, the locals were complaining about the cold, when it was 16°C.

I quickly told them they knew nothing about it!

But immersing yourself in icy water for an hour or two is something else altogether. Your body begins to shut down in that hostile environment.

Eventually, the guards told us we could come out. We were told to get dressed, and they led us over to a clearing, sat us down and, as we shivered, proceeded to debrief us. They said that we did not have enough respect for each other's abilities. In order for us to know how strong and powerful we were, they said, we were going to have to fight each other.

They had selected who was going to fight whom, and they gave us shorts, gloves and boxing headgear. We all sat around a clearing, forming a human ring, as the first two guys prepared to fight each other. Werner Greeff took on Thinus Delport. Each 'bout' was to consist of one round of three minutes.

Werner and Thinus started very meekly, tapping each other a few times, but not much more. The guards stopped the fight and said that if they messed around any more, they would have to spend the rest of the day running. 'Either hit each other properly or get punished,' the two were told.

Prompted by this warning, Thinus really climbed into Werner, getting in a good few shots. When it was over, Werner took off his gloves and threw them at the 'instructors' in disgust. He told them, 'This is really f***ed up.' His sentiments were shared by all of us.

Meanwhile, Rudolf Straeuli and Gideon Sam, our team manager, were observing everything. What is more, Rudi looked comfortable with the events taking place, and even announced who would fight whom. Another sadistic twist was pairing friend with friend. Hence, I was matched with Schalk Burger, and I went in with guns blazing, kicking and fighting. I thought, 'If he gets hold of me and hits me hard, he could knock me out.' Schalk is a big kid.

You were allowed only to punch each other, and by the end of our bout, Schalk had a bloody nose, which gave me not the slightest pleasure. But he was still young then; I wouldn't like to fight him now. Schalk showed me too much respect, but I realised very quickly that it was either him or me who was going to get bloodied. That was what our coach wanted; that was what he got.

Selborne Boome shuffled over to me on his backside and said, 'Look, I don't want to do this. Is it compulsory?' I told him I didn't think we'd be able to get out of it.

Gcobani Bobo knocked down Louis Koen three times. Then Danie Rossouw knocked Selborne Boome down with a massive blow. I was quite concerned about Selborne when he went down, but he quickly recovered. The Bulls players joked afterwards that it had been Danie Rossouw's first sober fight.

Selborne has mixed it among some of the toughest forwards in world rugby, including a spell in the French club game, where they certainly aren't pussycats. But the idea of fighting one of his own teammates repelled him. You could see he just didn't want to be anywhere near this distasteful affair.

I am no wimp either. I had laid my body on the line every time I left a changing room to run onto a rugby pitch. But this was unnecessarily cruel, and I felt sick for being a part of it. To this day, I simply cannot understand what they got out of it, to watch the World Cup squad knocking lumps out of each other until the blood flowed.

A great deal of comment was made about what really went

on at Kamp Staaldraad, most of it misinformed. The people who were talking or writing about it hadn't been there. They couldn't know what had happened at the camp. How could they begin to understand what the players went through and how they were humiliated?

The reason I am relating in such precise detail just what did happen is because I think people in South Africa should know what we went through. Even now I am still deeply unhappy about what had gone on at the camp.

If you've been a member of the Special Forces and have experience of this sort of training, I can understand that you might think you have to go through it in order to be a close-knit unit, to die for each other. But we weren't going to war; we were going to the Rugby World Cup, for heaven's sake. Our preparation time could have been used in so much more positive a manner than doing this.

While the boxing business was going on, I sat there thinking to myself that this was the most bizarre thing I had ever seen. I wished we didn't have to go through it. But I couldn't think of how to get out of it.

Again, I suppose I could have stood up and said, 'That's it, I am leaving. You can do what the hell you like, but I will have no further part of it.' I will always regret the fact that I didn't. What is equally hard to stomach is that I was probably too scared to take action. What if I threw away all I'd worked for? What if I threw away the chance to go to the World Cup if it was snatched from me a mere six weeks before the tournament started? The stakes were too high not to bite the bullet.

Today, I feel that I not only let myself down, but also my team-mates. Perhaps that is the toughest thing to have to live with. Good, decent people like Selborne Boome, Breyton Paulse, Louis Koen and the rest – I let them down, I failed them as a leader. I will always bitterly regret that. Certainly, standing up and saying, 'Count me out, I've had enough of this rubbish,' would have been extremely difficult in the circumstances. But I would have found it a lot easier to live with myself later, especially once I had retired and had time to think about it all. Frankly, the wound from that unhappy experience – and it was probably the worst experience of my entire playing career – stayed with me for a very long time. That might surprise some people, like Rudi Straeuli, but it is important that he knows that.

The whole exercise was demeaning, but of course that was the idea – to break us mentally, to humiliate and degrade us. Their ultimate goal was to see how we would react. But I didn't see any value in it then, and I still don't.

Players need to build up self-confidence, and that definitely wasn't on the agenda at this camp. You need self-belief, encouragement. Sure, there is value in taking players out of their comfort zone, just as there is in presenting a person with a challenge. But this was a perversion; it was totally over the top.

What enraged me as much as anything was to discover, some time later, that both the chief executive of SA Rugby, Rian Oberholzer, and Rudi Straeuli had known beforehand exactly what we would be put through. Oberholzer signed it off to the extent of R250 000, approving the plan in its entirety. When I discovered that, I was furious. I held them all responsible, not just Straeuli, but Oberholzer and, presumably, the other members of the board who must have been party to the decision. After all, should the entire board of SA Rugby not have approved such an expensive exercise?

Of course, it was the brainchild of Adriaan Heijns; we all knew that. I suppose part of it had to do with the 'macho' image of South African rugby. If we could go through Kamp Staaldraad and come out the other side, the theory went, just think what we could withstand on the rugby field. But the two have nothing to do with each other. The theory was absolute rubbish.

But that was not the full extent of what we went through during that miserable experience. Much, much more was to follow. And the worst was yet to come. We were ordered to march again, always carrying our individual rugby balls. But they were desperately difficult things to hold onto, because they weren't properly balanced. Water was slopping around inside each ball, and it was very easy to let it slip from your grasp. And the moment anyone dropped one, the punishments started again. Not to the individual who had dropped it. The guilty party had to stand and watch as everyone else was forced to do a gruelling set of push-ups. I suppose it was meant to teach you that your teammates would suffer if you made a mistake on the field. But there was no disguising the sadistic element attached to it.

More and more players started to drop the wretched rugby balls. As they grew more tired, their concentration lapsed, and down they went. We were stopping every few minutes to do push-ups. It was exhausting.

The march eventually took us back to base camp for the next task, an obstacle course. We were again split into three teams of ten, the forwards and backs being divided. We had one practice round, and then started. We'd been told that the team that won would get food. The losers would get nothing. We had not eaten a thing since we'd left Pretoria, about thirty-six hours earlier. By now it was early afternoon on the second day.

It was a long, difficult obstacle course, but my team did well and won. We were then given three little steel tins of lamb stew to share, and I told my team of ten to take a small mouthful and to give something to the other guys. They were sitting sullenly, watching us opening the tins. Joost didn't agree, and, quite honestly, what we were given wasn't enough for the ten of us, let alone another twenty. But we took a little of the food and passed it on. At least everyone had a bite. And I have to tell you, it tasted fantastic, just awesome.

The guards said we could lie down in the shade, and some of the guys immediately fell asleep, their rugby balls under their heads. We were an incredible sight: filthy, dirty, dishevelled, unshaven, of course, and faces and bodies blackened by dirt and sweat. Our shorts and tops were stained, filthy and torn. It was by now quite warm, maybe 30°C in the middle of the day. But the rest period did not last long.

We were roused from our slumber by the sound of gunshots. The next task was about to unfold. We were told a truck would transport us into the bush. We would be given a piece of wire, a one-inch-long match, a piece of wood, a knife – oh, and our wretched rugby balls. We couldn't go anywhere without those. We were also given a chicken leg and an egg. Of course, both were raw. They also took our shoes away, so that we were barefoot.

We were driven off five at a time, and dropped off individually. The knife's purpose was to carve something 'meaningful' out of the piece of wood. The match was to light a fire to keep us warm during the night, for by now the sun was beginning to set, and soon it would start to get very cold. There was plenty of wood in the bush, so we had to collect a pile to keep our fire going. If the fire went out or we didn't get it going with the tiny match, that would be it; we'd be out in the middle of the bush all night with no heat. The fire would also enable us to boil the egg and cook the chicken leg. But – and here was the next in the long line of sadistic twists – after you had cooked the chicken leg, you were not allowed to eat it. You had to take it back untouched the next day.

As soon as we were dropped off, I started to collect huge amounts of wood, which I thought would be more than enough for the night. And I did so with sheer delight. I was very happy to be on my own, let loose in the bush. I thought what a pleasure it was not to have to listen to the guards shouting and screaming at us any more.

I also picked up some dry grass and twisted it into a tight little bundle to ignite the fire once the match was struck. They had given us a little square piece of flint with which to light the match. You would only get one go at it; if your match failed or your fire did not catch quickly enough, that would be it. No fire all night. I had plenty of small twigs. I remember praying, 'Please God, let this thing light, because if it doesn't, I am going to freeze.'

I was exceedingly careful and very close to the grass when I lit the match. I was lying down over the grass, the match and flint literally touching the dry stalks, and when the match struck and the flame shot into the grass, causing it to shoot upwards, my hair and eyebrows got singed. I made two fires, one on either side of where I would lie, because I didn't want my back to get cold during the night.

Once the fires were going, I sat there thinking how good it was. This was what I loved doing: camping in the bush, listening to the cries of the occasional bird or animal far off. A wildebeest came to have a look at me, but was quickly scared away by the sight of the fire. It grew completely dark, and I sat there thinking about this mad escapade, and what might still lay ahead for us. But I was fortunate. I was a country boy who had grown up in the bush and was used to living in the wild. It was a pleasure for me. But for some of the other guys, especially those from the cities, it was another story. I knew that some of them had never stayed in the bush before.

As the fire continued to burn, I tied the chicken leg to a piece of wood and held it over the flames to cook it. After the chicken was more or less cooked, I dug a hole in the ground close to the fire and put my egg inside. I put soil over the top and urinated on it to create a little moist area, and then pushed some of the embers onto it so that it would boil the egg gradually. I made sure the egg was cooked hard and the chicken leg was also done. Then I fell asleep.

I don't know how much later it was, but it was still dark when I was woken by the sound of a truck drawing near. It was Rudi Straeuli and one of the guards. They asked me what time it was, and I thought that, because the moon had gone down, it would soon start getting light. Of course, that doesn't always apply, for the moon can go down at nine or ten at night. But I told them I estimated it was probably three or four in the morning. They just chuckled and left.

By this time the fire was starting to go out, and I had no more wood. So I broke a few branches off a tree close by and got it going again. The fire was essential, because this was the bush after all. Hyenas, snakes and other animals, like impala, lived in the area. The fire would scare them off.

I fell asleep again, and probably had another hour or two's rest. But then the truck returned, and we were picked up one by one to go back to base camp.

Before we were dropped off, the guards had warned us that we were not allowed to contact any other members of the squad. I couldn't hear anybody else during the night, but it was obvious they couldn't have been too far away, as there'd been five of us on the back of the truck. I assumed the other guys were in the vicinity. But we were strictly forbidden to try to find each other.

When we got back to base camp, they lined us up and announced that one member of the squad, Dale Santon, had indeed walked through the bush to find a colleague. He had lost his match and wanted to get some fire for the night. Therefore, we were told, we were all going to be punished. Frankly, I didn't resent Dale, as I would have done the same in the circumstances.

So we all had to do another set of push-ups. But by that time, I was in survival mode; I didn't care any more. I was used to the bush and didn't fear anything out there. I knew I had the skills to handle the environment. And being in survival mode helped me believe I could get through this experience, no matter what they threw at us.

When the sun came up, everyone looked in a terrible state. The smoke of the fires had blackened our faces, and together with the two days we'd had without being able to wash, we were a pitiful sight. It looked funny, in fact, and it surprised me that we could still laugh at such a time.

We had to show the 'instructors' our egg, chicken leg and carving. A couple of guys had eaten their chicken leg, and a few of the eggs were broken. Each of us had to step forward, and one of the guards took your egg and promptly smashed it on your head to check whether it was cooked. A lot of guys had under-cooked their eggs, and when they were smashed on their heads, the yolk trickled down their faces, mingling with the dust, soot and sweat. I could see that Selborne Boome was deeply upset and humiliated by this scene, and I didn't blame him.

Those of us who had cooked the chicken leg and egg properly were allowed to eat both. But when one has not eaten much for the best part of two days, one gets past the point of hunger. You may need water to survive, but the body loses the desire for food. And they did give us more than enough water.

With this little charade behind us, we were marched back to the water. We thought, 'Oh, no, not in there again.' But this time we had to build a raft, and they gave us four drums, two poles and loads of rope. But you had a limited time in which to do this. My group did extremely well and built a very solid raft, perhaps because a few of us, like Richard Bands and myself, were farm boys and knew how to do such things. But again, some of the city boys struggled. We then had to take a raft about a hundred yards across the water, and the team that won would be given four chocolate bars.

But before we set off, there was another little twist. You couldn't take the raft you had built; you had to take one made by another group. So, for example, the first group took the third group's raft and the second group took the first group's. One group's raft was a disaster, and started falling apart halfway across the lake. They came stone last and arrived soaking wet and freezing cold once again. The group that got our raft won. They shared the chocolate bars, so that everybody had a taste.

But before that small pleasure, there were more of the usual punishments for making 'mistakes': crawling around on the ground, doing push-ups, et cetera.

Then they asked the guys who had eaten their chicken legs to step forward. I hadn't eaten mine, but they said I hadn't done my push-ups properly, so I had to join the others in the group. And guess what, we were going to be punished again.

We were shown some old ammunition boxes, which had been filled with cement. In addition to the box, we were given a steel railway track, which in turn had a huge ball and chain attached. We were told that we would have to carry this contraption. The ball alone was heavier than the steel tracks. We had to walk up a hill and back, which we did until we were so shattered we didn't care about anything any more. And if someone put any of these huge, unbalanced weights down, they were hammered with more physical punishments like push-ups, and more shouting and screaming, which seemed to go on most of the time.

When we had finished this gruelling exercise, we had to stand up and sing the national anthem. One exhausted guy nearly fainted. By this time, some of the younger guys, like Derick Hougaard, were really struggling to survive. But I noticed that most of the Blue Bulls guys, the typical Afrikaners, were able to keep going. Maybe that ability was as much mental as physical in nature.

We were then told we would be given GPS systems and had to make our way back to base camp. We would take the direct route through the bush to find our way back. So we set off, but, after about twenty minutes, Victor Matfield suddenly realised he had left his GPS behind. We knew there would be a huge punishment if we didn't retrieve it, so a couple of the guys went back with Victor. The rest of us waited in the bush, and it was fine there. As long as they weren't screaming and shouting at us, we felt okay.

Eventually we went on, and reached the point where we had to be. It was just a clearing in the bush, but there was a tree hut close by, and Neil de Kock climbed up to peep inside. Suddenly a gun was poked against his forehead by the guard hiding in the hut, from where he was obviously spying on us.

And then we found some crates of beer lying around nearby. Now what do you do? By this time, dirty, dishevelled and worn out, we could have murdered a few beers. But we knew what the cost would be, because it hadn't been approved. It was just another of their many nasty tricks, to tempt us to have some beers and then cop more punishment. You could read these guys' minds like you read a book. They were that predictable. So we left the beers alone and just sat down and waited.

We knew the guard was eavesdropping, so we sat whispering together for some time. After what seemed like ages, the guards appeared with a rope. A mock hanging this time? By this stage, I wouldn't have put anything past them, but it turned out to be a lot simpler: a tug-of-war contest. Oh, and the team that won would get food. Again. We were getting used to this nonsense.

But what followed was really twisted, even by their standards. My team won the tug-of-war, and the guards brought out a huge box. At last, I thought, proper food. This is when we *really* eat. But I should have known them by now.

Inside the box were three live chickens. They took them out, handed the chickens to three carefully selected guys – John Smit, Joe van Niekerk and Derick Hougaard – and said, 'Kill it.'

Joe had never killed anything in his life and was very tense. Having grown up on a farm, I knew how to kill a chicken: you put the head between your fingers and just twist it in one quick movement. If you have the correct technique, it is simple, straightforward and does not cause the bird any pain.

But Joe didn't have the technique. Clearly upset, he became almost paranoid and ended up smashing the bird on the ground, trying to finish it off. The poor chicken took a while to complete its death throes and finally lay still. I sat there watching this, feeling angry and ashamed. It was horrible and disgusting and very harsh on Joe. I felt very sorry for him. All these things had nothing to do with preparing for a Rugby World Cup. It had gone far beyond anything remotely connected with a sports tournament. We'd been lured into a world of sadism, where almost every sick trick could be enacted on us. I looked around at my fellow players and I thought to myself, 'What a mess, what a nightmare, and I am part of it. This is a sick, degrading exercise, and we shouldn't have been brought anywhere near it.'

When the birds were dead, we owned all three as the winning team. Which meant that fifteen guys were facing the prospect of watching us eat. So we split the chickens between groups of ten, giving each group one each. We plucked the birds, took the biggest one for ourselves, which I thought was fair, and cooked it over an open fire. But the decision was flawed: the biggest chicken was a tough old thing and would, had it not crossed the Springbok squad's path, probably have died of old age in the not-too-distant future. We could hardly eat it. The point of my knife could hardly get into the flesh, and our group went hungry.

We were allowed to rest or sleep for a while, before they woke us a short time later and took us to a hole. We had to take off all our kit and crawl naked through a pipe, ending up in a big pit that was covered by a tarpaulin. The video footage that was taken here would cause an outcry when still photographs taken from it appeared in the South African media.

The guard told us that this was an opportunity to discuss any problems we had within the team, to bring them out into the open. Ashwin Willemse was quite vocal, and said that Joost treated him in a very racist manner. I was the mediator and tried to intervene. A few things were said, and then the New Zealand *haka* was played at us, blasting out over loudspeakers close by. It was a deafening noise. It was pitch-black in the pit, you couldn't see your hand in front of you, but then they would suddenly pull back the tarpaulin and shine torches in our eyes, blinding us. All the time, the *haka* pounded out from the speakers. I estimated they played it forty times, but it could have been a lot more. It was bewildering, and we were sick of hearing it. And, just to complete their enjoyment, we were then hosed down with cold water, leaving us sitting there, shivering.

I don't know how long we spent in the pit, but by now it was probably the middle of the night. They told us we could get out and put our shorts on, but not shoes or a shirt. Then they marched us down the road, told us to lie on our backs and gave us a talk on the stars. I was so cold, I was holding onto Dale Santon for warmth. Everybody was knackered, as we hadn't slept properly for about three days by this time. But the guard kept warning us that if we fell asleep, we would be punished.

We lay there, perhaps for an hour, before they got us up and marched us around some more. They didn't let us sleep at all that night. The next morning, we were taken to a truck that was parked in a field, which we had to push for I don't know how long or how far. By now, we were numb with tiredness. Our brains weren't really functioning properly. We were short of food, sleep, everything. After pushing the truck for ages, we were told to get on board, and they took us to a place where we would participate in climbing, abseiling and paint-balling. We abseiled down the rocks, but we had to climb a massive hill to get to the top first.

But before that happened, there was yet another mental test we had to pass. The guards took us into a room, and inside a buffet breakfast had been laid out. It was a lovely spread. Our eyes sparkled at the sight of it. But this was just a part of their mind games. The guards said, 'You can eat if you want – it is your decision.' The implied threat was unmistakeable. So a few of us senior guys said that it wasn't worth it, as we'd get punished again. It was a big decision to make after almost three days of going hungry. But we each took one apple or a banana and made do with that. Most of the food remained untouched.

The next exercise involved groups of seven or eight of us

being flown in a military helicopter over the lake. The helicopter would hover about twenty metres above the surface, and we had to jump out into the water. It was pretty unnerving, but we did it. The shock of the cold water on hitting the surface was extreme. We got out of the water freezing cold again, and had to march back to the camp. By now, it was late morning. When we arrived, there was a big tent. They told us we had five minutes to get in there and sleep for an hour. We dived into the tent and collapsed. I fell asleep with my head resting on someone's stomach. No one cared, we were just so tired.

When the guards woke us up, we were told we could have a shower, one minute under the water per person. It was hardly enough time to clean ourselves properly, considering we were covered in three days' worth of grime and muck. But we did what we could, and afterwards were given a clean T-shirt and tracksuit bottoms to wear. There was a massive fire going in the camp, and we were given bottles of Coke and beer, and steaks to cook. I drank plenty of Coke before having a beer, but those who drank a beer or two first were given a verbal hammering by Gideon Sam. He said that although the camp had been very tough, some of us had to show more discipline instead of going straight for the beer. He threw quite a tantrum – it was most bizarre and, I thought, totally unnecessary.

I can't even remember feeling relieved that it was all over. I was too tired to feel anything. All I wanted was to slake my thirst, eat a decent meal and then have a good, long sleep.

The next morning, we were driven out of the camp and back to the High Performance Centre. We each enjoyed a very long shower and put some proper clothes on again.

That is exactly what went on at Kamp Staaldraad, almost every detail. And, in hindsight, I am convinced that it was of no value whatsoever. What we went through was a complete waste of time. In our quest to win the Rugby World Cup, it didn't make any difference at all. Indeed, after the tournament, some people used the camp as an excuse for why we *lost* the World Cup. I never agreed with that, but I certainly did not agree with the concept of the camp as part of our preparation either. Not at all.

Later, we found that the footage taken of us naked in that pit had been blasted around the world, and I was very upset about it. Dale McDermott was our video analyst, and he had filmed most of the incidents at the camp. I don't know why he was allowed to be there when Gert Smal and Ray Mordt had been sent home. I assumed Rudi Straeuli did not want them there. At the time, I thought it was bizarre to film the incidents. It might have been acceptable – just – had those images been retained forever within South African rugby circles. But then the *Cape Argus* got hold of them, having allegedly 'acquired' them for R50 000. We were absolutely furious when we heard about it, and when we saw the outcome, we felt betrayed.

Clearly, Dale McDermott forever after regretted allowing those images to enter the public domain. He lost his job with SA Rugby. Then, while I was at Northampton in the winter of 2004/05, we were coming home on a coach from an away match when Frank Ponissi, who was one of our back-up coaching members, walked down the bus and handed me his cellphone. There was a message on it from the reporter who had bought the footage from Dale, which read: 'Dale McDermott has just blown his brains out.' Nothing else. I thought it was a particularly crude way to inform Dale's former colleagues of his death.

At the inquest, an open verdict was recorded. The loss of his job and guilt at having sold the Staaldraad video footage seemed to have contributed to Dale McDermott's decision to commit suicide.

When I look back, I realise that Kamp Staaldraad was just Rudi Straeuli clutching at straws. He was in a desperate situation, probably realising that he didn't have the players or the game plan with which to win the World Cup. He listened to people who proposed doing something entirely new, something radical as part of our preparation. Of course, it was absolute nonsense, complete rubbish. Sure, it made us suffer for seventy-two hours, but for what? We didn't play any better because of it, nor did it improve our team spirit.

Things hadn't gone well for Rudi during his time as Bok coach, and he probably knew what was coming at the World Cup. The mistake he made was to allow himself to be influenced by those who had proposed the Staaldraad idea. I do not believe that it was Rudi who had come up with the plan originally. He listened to others. But, in the end, what happened at that camp brought down both Rudi Straeuli and Rian Oberholzer.

My abiding memory of our time at the camp was that I let my players down by not helping them enough in that time of adversity. I will always struggle with that fact. When I talked about the camp for this book, I felt as if I was appearing in front of Archbishop Desmond Tutu at the Truth and Reconciliation Commission. It was a cathartic experience for me, because not even my wife knew the details of Kamp Staaldraad before this book. I never told her what had really gone on. Perhaps I felt ashamed about my part in it, and the way I felt I had failed the players.

I know today I should have stood up for them, and every time I spoke about the camp afterwards, I felt guilty. I suppose that was why I never told Justine, and generally hated discussing it. It was a stain on my Springbok career, something I had been so hugely proud of. I felt as if I had been brainwashed, which was one of the hardest things to live with.

I will always bitterly regret that I did not stand up and say, 'Listen, you can do what you like. I am taking my thirty players off this camp.' I should have done it, but I didn't. Rugby players have rights, just like anyone else. They have their dignity, and they should be able to retain it while training to represent their country. Deliberately degrading and dehumanising athletes should have no place in any sporting team's preparations. We are entitled to point a very accusing finger at those who ran SA Rugby at the time just for the fact that our basic human rights were denied us at that camp. What we endured at Kamp Staaldraad, the verbal, mental and physical abuse, had nothing to do with what we should have been about, namely preparing for a Rugby World Cup. The intention of the camp was intrinsically wrong, because players need to be built up and given confidence to make them believe they can be champions. At that camp, they only tried to break us down. They said, 'You never know how tough you can be until you are broken. Now win the World Cup.'

It doesn't make any sense. We may have been fit at the World Cup, but we were also mentally tired during the tournament.

Rian Oberholzer only had himself to blame for losing his job. He should have stopped the camp. He should have had the foresight and vision to know that the pride of the nation in terms of rugby should not be compromised before the most important tournament of the players' lives.

I will always feel sadness and disappointment that the biggest moment of my rugby career, leading the Springboks in a World Cup tournament, was messed up by a few horrible days in the bush. No player should go through that.

Above all, Kamp Staaldraad allowed certain people's bizarre ideas to hold sway over common sense and the sanctity of others' human rights. And that has to be a matter of eternal regret to the good name of South African rugby.

8
In Search of the Holy Grail: The 2003 World Cup

When Rudolf Straeuli announced his squad to go to Australia in October 2003 for the fifth Rugby World Cup, just seven of the twenty-eight players who had participated in the tour to France, Scotland and England at the end of 2002 were chosen in the thirty-man party. In other words, in a little less than ten months, Straeuli had rejected or was unable to select twenty-one players who had made that tour. So startling a turnover of players so close to a World Cup hardly bode well for our chances in the tournament.

What is more, for the fifth year in succession, South Africa had finished the Tri-Nations competition bottom of the table, with just one win from four matches. We beat Australia 26-22 at Cape Town, but the other home game in the Tri-Nations ended in the notorious 16-52 defeat to New Zealand in Pretoria. In that game, we matched the New Zealand forwards, but they hit a purple patch and carved us up in the backs. Our defence was poor too.

I played in the entire 2003 Super 12 tournament, but for the Stormers it wasn't a particularly successful season, and we failed to reach the semi-finals. We didn't deserve to qualify for the play-offs, either. Nor was there much joy for Western Province in the Currie Cup. We were in the midst of the Blue Bulls' ascendancy. They had followed our brace of titles in 2000 and 2001 by winning the trophy in 2002 and 2003, as they were to do in 2004.

It wasn't a happy international year for the Springboks leading up to the World Cup. With the sour taste of that end-of-year tour in 2002 still lingering, we prepared to face Scotland, who were making a two-test tour of the Republic. It was obviously a chance to take revenge for our defeat in Edinburgh a few months earlier, but, more importantly, also an opportunity for Straeuli to put together the kind of side he had in mind for the World Cup, and familiarise the players with playing together. After the two Scottish tests, we were due to meet Argentina at home before starting preparations for the Tri-Nations.

The good news was that we won our first four internationals of that year, both the Scottish tests, the Argentine game and then Australia at home. But win/loss ratios can fool you. The story behind those games didn't deceive anyone.

We struggled past Scotland in Durban, winning 29-25, then came with a late rush of points to beat them, again unconvincingly, 28-19 in Johannesburg, and then we had the mother of all frights in beating Argentina 26-25 in Port Elizabeth, thanks to a last-minute penalty from Louis Koen. Argentina played their usual disruptive game and were on fire, but it was still alarming that we couldn't master them throughout the match. But they can make life very difficult for their opponents, as Ireland discovered in the 1999 World Cup. Six years later, the British & Irish Lions experienced something similar when they played the Pumas in Cardiff before leaving on their ill-fated tour of New Zealand. They could only scramble a 25-all draw through a last-minute Jonny Wilkinson penalty.

But, in truth, none of our performances at that time had any conviction to them, and the side was constantly chopped and changed. Obviously Rudi Straeuli wasn't happy with what his teams were producing, as his frequent changes revealed. Or was he perhaps doubting his own judgement?

Whatever the reason, it seemed to me that he couldn't make a decision on whom he wanted to play. But the more he meddled and changed the team, the more it cut down our chances in the World Cup. Any side that wants to go to a World Cup with a hope of winning it has to be a settled unit. They must have long since figured out their best side, and worked hard on creating combinations and partnerships among players in key positions.

For example, fly half Louis Koen played almost throughout the 2003 season, winning the starting No. 10 jersey against Scotland twice, Argentina, New Zealand home and away, and Australia away. Rudi started the World Cup with him as first choice, but after the defeat by England, promptly dropped him in favour of Derick Hougaard of the Blue Bulls.

My contention was that you can't keep swapping players around before or during a World Cup, not unless you have a 'gimme' type of fixture, such as one against Namibia or Uruguay. In those circumstances, you obviously take the chance to rest some of your more established stars and give the remaining squad guys a game. But Koen was dropped to the bench for the vital match against Samoa at the World Cup.

Of course, there was another reason why Rudi changed his teams around so much. He said that he never wanted the players to feel that the jersey belonged to them. He preferred a situation in which everyone had to go out and earn it every single time they played.

To some extent, I could understand his philosophy. The Springbok jersey is bigger than any one player, and if someone is better than another player, then he should be selected. But he should play consistently in that position, and a coach should use the four years between World Cups to decide which players are the best in their positions. And, most crucial of all, once you have made your decision, you must stand by it. You have to give the player time to adapt to his role, to feel comfortable, assured and settled, so that he can then produce his best form.

Players fearing the axe generally play safe; they risk nothing. They play within themselves, try very little and are often no threat to the opposition. But those players who have worked hard to prove themselves and make the jersey their own can concentrate fully on beating their opponents and helping their teammates win the game. They won't do so if they are constantly worrying that one mistake might cost them their place.

Unfortunately, that was the feeling that existed for too long in Straeuli's sides leading up to the 2003 World Cup. Hardly anyone was sure of his place. I could see what Rudi was trying to do, but in my book, it went too far as a policy. At some stage, Rudi had to say, 'This is my first-choice XV,' and stuck with them. But he never really did.

I found that Rudi became increasingly withdrawn as 2003 progressed and the World Cup drew closer. It didn't take a genius to see that he was beginning to suffer under the pressure, just as every Springbok coach does at some stage. That is as certain as night following day. The pressures of the coach's job are enormous. There are millions of people in the country who would swear on their mother's life that they know far more about rugby football than the national coach. They'll debate the coach's team selections into the small hours, arguing endlessly about combinations, individuals and tactics.

'*Ag* man, that back-rower, he can't catch a ball and he certainly won't run for more than half the game – what the heck is he doing in the team?' And so on and so on.

It is all very healthy and to be encouraged – in one respect. We South Africans simply love the game. No, let me correct that. We are obsessed with it. Rugby is an ongoing love affair that rages throughout our lives. We experience huge highs, passionate moments of great joy and pleasure, followed not long after by desperate lows, plunging us into the depths of despair. And all this over a game of rugby! But that's the way we are – a people who adore this game. And long may it continue, I say. But, at the same time, this public obsession leads to tremendous pressure on the coach. And not everyone can handle that …

Rudi Straeuli had his own ideas on team selection and, although it was obvious he was concerned, he didn't let on very much or discuss many aspects of it with me. I think he should have. If a coach doesn't communicate his feelings and thoughts to his captain, it makes it much more difficult for him out on the field during a match. The captain has to make quick decisions, dictated by events on the field, and if he hasn't got a clue what his coach's thoughts are on the issue, then it's like taking a stab in the dark.

But Rudi was too inclined to bottle up his problems. It wasn't good for him or for the team. I wanted to help; I was certainly ready to do so as captain. But I didn't feel he was taking me into his confidence, and in a sense it left a void between the Springbok coach and his captain – not an ideal situation.

Because Rudi was under such huge pressure, he tended to vent his frustrations on the team. I began to see that the more pressure he suffered, the more control he wanted over us, both as a team and as individuals. He tried to control us totally: our rugby lives, our social lives, everything.

I suspect that Rudi felt if he could control us totally as players, then perhaps he could have a bigger influence on the results of the games. But it was the wrong way to go about preparing for a World Cup.

Rudi has a very dry sense of humour, but the guys often didn't get his jokes. They weren't always sure whether he was making a joke or an insinuation, with the result that it often fell flat.

I got the impression that Rudi was listening to the wrong people. And they tended to make him a bit paranoid, which meant that everyone and everything suffered because of that. To be honest, never at any stage did I think the Springboks would have a settled side for the World Cup.

One of the guys who might have expected to be at the World Cup, Pedrie Wannenberg, the back row player from the Blue Bulls, did not go, and it was because of me. Pedrie was in the squad for the Tri-Nations test match against New Zealand in Pretoria before the World Cup. We arrived at the ground, put our bags down and went out onto the field. I strolled around for a short time, but as I was coming off the field to go back into the changing room, I noticed Pedrie. He was on his cellphone, and it turned out he was talking to his girlfriend. I had nothing against the guy, but I just felt he was abusing the Springbok jersey. If you can't be more focused than that less than an hour before a test match against New Zealand, then you don't understand the way international rugby works. It was positively dangerous for team spirit.

When I tackled him about it later, he said it was part of his preparation for the game. I just lost it and said, 'Don't bullshit me.' But I don't think he was that bothered – he didn't understand the seriousness of the situation. I felt Pedrie wasn't good for team spirit, and I had enough other issues to worry about.

Some time later, when Rudi Straeuli was in the process of selecting his squad for the World Cup, I went to see him. I said, 'Look, I have never done anything like this before, but I don't want to go to the World Cup with this guy. I think Schalk Burger can be of immense value at the World Cup.'

Should the coach have listened to me? Yes, I think so. In a way I felt bad about it, but I didn't think I was wrong, and I still don't. And the player we took instead turned out to be a fantastic performer.

The way the draw had been made, it was obvious that we had to beat England in our pool match at the Subiaco Oval, Perth, on 18 October, if we wanted to make significant progress in the tournament. Our World Cup would come down to whether we could get past a side that, eleven months earlier, had wiped the floor with us at Twickenham. If we could, the road to the semi-finals would open up, because I was sure that with our fighting spirit we would beat Samoa, also in Pool C, and then we would in all likelihood face Wales in the quarter-finals. I knew we could beat them, and if we reached the semi-finals of the World Cup, well, anything was possible. But fifteen guys in white shirts barred our way.

Quite honestly, I have to say that I never felt certain that I was the captain of a potential World Cup–winning team. England and New Zealand had beaten us by fifty points in the previous twelve months; in New Zealand's case, it was at Pretoria in the Tri-Nations barely three months earlier. But my heart told me nothing was impossible. If we wore the Springbok jersey with pride and spirit, as I knew we would, anything was possible. But my head told me that we just weren't ready for this World Cup. We didn't have a settled side, and we didn't have the overall quality of teams that, for example, England and New Zealand had. You cannot go to a World Cup and just hope that, magically, everything turns out all right in those four to six weeks. You can't miraculously change a team that has been roundly defeated by two other leading rugby nations into world-beaters. It simply doesn't work like that. Perhaps, given the success of 2004, we were a year too early.

Everyone knows what happened in the end, so I don't want to spend too much time recounting the details. But overall, I enjoyed the World Cup; I enjoyed being in the tournament as a player. There was a great atmosphere wherever you went in Australia. I think, subconsciously, I had made a decision to just take pleasure in it. After all, this was rugby's Olympics, and players should make the most of it, whatever the eventual fate of their team.

Australia was a great country in which to hold the World Cup. If the 2000 Sydney Olympics had been the best ever, then perhaps the 2003 Rugby World Cup was the best so far. Of course, every South African will feel a strong attachment to the 1995 tournament, which we hosted and won. But the World Cup has grown enormously since we staged it a decade ago. It is bigger and glitzier, has more meaning, greater importance and altogether more razzle-dazzle. The levels of interest in it right around the world are now enormous.

Initially we were based in Perth, where we met England, and later moved to Sydney and Melbourne. We enjoyed Perth. I remember the location we called 'Cappucino Lane', an area of the city that had streets filled with numerous coffee bars. We used to sit in one of the cafes and chill out when we'd finished training, drinking coffee and playing cards. In one game, the purpose was to get rid of our cards. The first guy to do so was king; the last, an arsehole! We spent a lot of time playing cards.

The pool match against England was one we could have won. We were right in it at half-time, but Louis Koen missed some crucial kicks and then had a clearance kick charged down, which resulted in England centre Will Greenwood scoring a vital try under the posts. That knocked us right back, and although Victor Matfield continued to win us copious amounts of line-out ball, the fact was England were more settled as a side than us, and in a tight game, that counted. They also had more self-belief, and that, too, came through in the end. Self-belief doesn't materialise during the course of one match; it develops over a period of time. Players gradually learn to believe in one another, and then, no matter what the score, you believe you can pull something out of the bag.

At one stage in that match, the score was 6-all, and it appeared to be anyone's game. But you always sensed that England's greater cohesion, and the fact that they'd spent so much more time together as a side, would prove crucial. And that was what happened in the end.

Behind the scenes, there was a drama that few knew about on the day. Louis Koen's wife, who was pregnant, had been held up at gunpoint in Johannesburg by thugs who stole her handbag. It was a very traumatic time for them both, and Louis' game might well have suffered as a result. I am sure it disrupted his preparation because of the sleepless nights he endured. But, having said that, on the day it just didn't work out for us.

Bakkies Botha was another player who had a big game for us against England. When you looked at our two locks, you knew we had the basis on which to build a formidable forward unit for the future. Both were at the right ages, Victor at twenty-six and Bakkies at twenty-four, to play for years at the heart of the Springbok pack. In fact, the Springbok pack played well as a unit that day. But it wasn't enough.

One thing I figured out during my time as an international rugby player was that certain teams know how to beat each other. Australia know how to beat New Zealand, New Zealand know how to beat England, and South Africa know how to beat the Aussies. Don't ask me why – it's weird. But if you page through the history books of this sport, you will find that I am right. Perhaps players have more belief when they play certain teams; maybe certain sides have your number.

Certainly, I think New Zealand would have beaten England to win the tournament. But in the event, Australia figured the Kiwis out in the semi-final, winning 22-10.

Throughout the build-up to that World Cup, Rudi Straeuli was working hard to try to gain any sort of psychological advantage he could find for us. He put English jerseys with the names of their players on all our tackle bags, so we'd hit Jonny Wilkinson like hell in training, with a kind of 'take that, pal' attitude.

However, I always felt that Rudi was building up the England game to such an extent that, if we lost it, the players would basically feel our World Cup was over. But, credit to the players, I never sensed this after our 6-25 loss against England in Perth. We held our heads high for the remainder of the tournament.

Our spirits were raised when Samoa nearly beat England, going down 22-35 in the end, but we gave them an absolute hiding six days later, winning 60-10 at the Suncorp Stadium in Brisbane. But they'd probably given their all against England and didn't have a lot left in the tank when we played them. Remember, there was a lot of criticism from the so-called smaller nations that they had been presented with ridiculous schedules by the organisers. Samoa, for example, had to play four test matches in seventeen days, Italy four tests in just fourteen days, and one of them against New Zealand! That was a crazy schedule and totally unfair. No wonder the Italians threatened never to take part in another World Cup if they were ever presented with such a schedule again.

We had settled into our hotel in Melbourne prior to the

quarter-final game against New Zealand. One day, at lunch, the squad was served thirty eggs and thirty drumsticks. That was all. Naturally, the first players to arrive in the dining room ate the lot. There was nothing left for the rest of us. I asked Rudi whether we could order more food, and he said no. He thought the players were becoming too complacent, settling back into their old ways. The food had been intended to remind us that, as players in a team, we were supposed to look out for each other. I thought it odd to deprive your players of vital sustenance before a World Cup quarter-final game against the All Blacks …

A few days later, we played New Zealand in the quarter-final. The lack of self-belief in certain players cost us dearly, and we were hammered. For most of their rugby careers, these players had lost to New Zealand, and you just sensed a feeling of 'here we go again' when the All Blacks scored.

We sat in the changing room after our 9-29 defeat in Melbourne, and Victor Matfield looked across at me. 'What are you going to do now?' he asked.

'Retire,' I said.

Joost van der Westhuizen had announced that it would be his last game for the Boks, and I had had enough too. I had only played in three matches at the World Cup – England, Samoa and New Zealand – and as I sat in that dressing room, I felt totally deflated. Victor said to me, 'I'm very sorry, I feel that I and a few of the guys let you down.'

I told him that nobody goes out to try to lose in a Springbok jersey, and he had tried his best. But it was really nice of him to say that.

I told Rudi Straeuli, 'That's it as far as I'm concerned.' But he said, 'No, no. I want you to stay another year and bring John Smit through as captain.' That did interest me, and I remember saying to Justine that I would play through to the end of the Tri-Nations in 2004, and then Smit would take over as captain for the end-of-year tour to Europe.

But I seriously underestimated the turmoil that broke within South African rugby as a result of our failure to win the World Cup. Within weeks, certainly months, people were being fired left, right and centre. My contract ended after the World Cup, yet Rian Oberholzer backed Straeuli's view, telling me he thought I should stay for another year. He even went so far as to say to me, 'When you have time, come to my office at Newlands and sign a one-year contract.' It was that explicit.

But the mumbles and grumbles within South African rugby were growing by the day. The guns turned on Rudi Straeuli, and rumours began to fly that he and Rian Oberholzer might be fired. I said to Justine, 'I should go and sign the new contract before Rian is fired, or it will be the end of me too.'

But Justine wisely asked, 'Do you think that is the right thing to do?'

And that set me thinking. If both Straeuli and Oberholzer were fired, where would that leave me? I'd captained the team to the World Cup, and I knew I had plenty of enemies – people within South African rugby who would delight in pushing me out. With both Straeuli and Oberholzer gone, I would surely be the next to go. Why would the coach and chief executive be fired and the captain retained? It didn't make any sense, especially as events at Twickenham in 2002 had created enemies for me within official circles of our game. I knew that, and I understood the unwritten rules.

I thought it over and eventually said to Justine, 'If Rian phones again, I will go and sign the contract. Otherwise, I'll forget it.'

Then, two weeks later, Straeuli and Rian resigned. He hadn't called me again.

Just after that, I went to Newlands to the Sports Science Institute to train one day. As I arrived, they happened to be carrying Rian's files out to his car. Soon after, Rian appeared. I stuck my hand out and just said, 'Hard lines.' I did it because I had respect for him and wanted to commiserate.

His face coloured. He turned and said to me somewhat curtly, 'This is what you players wanted.'

I replied, 'Possibly, but I wanted you to know how I feel.'

Rian looked at me for a moment, and then said, 'You were stupid. You should have come in and signed that contract when I offered it to you.'

My reply was brief: 'Rian, that's not the way I do business.'

It wasn't about the money. If they'd fired me, which they were likely to do with Rudi and Rian gone, they would have had to pay me off. I'd have a twelve-month contract, despite knowing they wanted me out. I would in effect have been saying to them, 'Well, you've got to pay me a year's money for doing nothing before I'll go. Otherwise I'll sue.'

I hoped I was a better person than that.

Oberholzer and Straeuli had paid the price for Kamp Staaldraad – I had been Straeuli's captain. Why on earth would SA Rugby have retained me other than to avoid paying me out for my new contract? It would have made me feel like a fraud, hanging on just for the money. It was better to be honest, face the truth that my time was over and that I had to move on.

To this day, I remember Justine's wise words, and I am deeply grateful to her for making me stop and think things through. I didn't want sainthood, because I wasn't a saint as a rugby player. But I didn't want to be remembered as a swindler, as someone who would sell his soul for a sum of money when he was, in fact, no longer wanted. It wasn't the way I wanted to end my rugby career.

I think it is true to say that when somebody is in a job, you don't always appreciate them as you should. This was perhaps the case with Rian Oberholzer. Not until he left was he perhaps really appreciated. I had a few things to thank him for. He saved me from a major IRB disciplinary hearing, which could have been ruinous to my career, and I am forever grateful to him for that.

As for Straeuli, SA Rugby had to find a way to get him to

resign. Kamp Staaldraad was their ticket out, as Rudi did not have a performance clause in his contract with SA Rugby. They therefore couldn't fire him on his bad results at the World Cup, and a golden handshake would have been far too costly. Instead, they used Staaldraad as an excuse to get rid of him.

To complete the bloodletting, Silas Nkanunu was voted out as president. It had been some purge. Who was next? The captain? I decided to jump before I was pushed.

In the end, I am glad I resigned, especially as Jake White took over as Springbok coach. I would have had no future under him. When I was Springbok captain, he coached the Under 21s, and before that, when Nick Mallett was Springbok coach, Jake was the video analyst. I enjoyed his company then, and found him really friendly. But not that long after he took over the Under 21s, he wrote in the papers that I wasn't the right guy for Springbok captain. He said he wouldn't have me as his skipper, and that John Smit would make a much better captain.

Everyone is entitled to his or her opinion, but in my book, if you are employed by the South African Rugby Football Union, you don't publicly criticise the Springbok captain. I took exception to that. I hadn't had good results as skipper; that was undeniably true. But I still felt it was unnecessary for him to state so publicly. If I have a problem with someone, I will seek him or her out to discuss the matter in private. I will not make my views known through the papers.

I am the sort of person who wears his heart on his sleeve, but in this instance I didn't think it appropriate to react to Jake's criticisms. I just got on with the job. But when Rudolf Straeuli resigned and the talk was that Jake might replace him, I knew there would be no future for me under him.

But you never stop learning lessons in life. One day, at the SARFU offices at Newlands, I saw Jake coming down the corridor. As he approached, I walked straight past him without saying a word. Neither of us spoke. And that was the last time

I saw Jake White, really, when I had an opportunity to talk to him.

Perhaps, looking back now, I had acted childishly; I should have been more mature about it. If I had stopped, he would probably have greeted me. But you do things in life that you regret afterwards. At the time, I didn't suddenly want to be friendly to him just because he might be the next Springbok coach. I'm not a hypocrite. I have no ongoing axe to grind with Jake, and I was as delighted as any South African when he steered the Boks to their 2004 Tri-Nations success.

Looking back on my career, I wouldn't want anyone to think that I was ever arrogant. I hope no one I played against ever said that about me. Maybe I didn't always agree with other guys' opinions, but I was always there for the players. Whatever they wanted, I tried to get for them. But I admit that, under Rudi Straeuli, I didn't do enough of that. I didn't fight for the players enough, and that is the one thing I regret in my time as Springbok captain. I believe I failed them in that respect, and yet I am still not sure why.

At the end of the day, I'd had enough of being Springbok captain, and that was another big deciding factor in quitting international rugby. I suppose, with hindsight, if I'd thought there was change for the good on the horizon, and I could see a huge improvement coming in the near future, I might have hung in there. After all, I was still only twenty-eight. That is quite early to quit international rugby. But in the months that followed, I never regretted my decision. It would not have worked out to stick around into another era. I'd have ended up walking away with my tail between my legs, and as anyone who knows me would tell you, that isn't my style.

It was the end of an era when the World Cup was over. Rian and Rudi resigned their jobs; Joost and I packed up. That was the way it was, and it was better for me that it happened like that.

I was left to reflect on the frustrations of the 2003 World Cup. There were matches we'd lost that we might have won, but in the end, the bottom line was that we just hadn't been good enough.

England went on to win the trophy, the reward for the consistency of their selections over the preceding couple of years. Their coach, Clive Woodward, had had a long time to build towards that moment; after all, he'd been in charge when we beat them at the 1999 World Cup in Paris. Despite a clamour on the part of some people in the UK to sack him after that failure, Woodward stayed on and, four years later, English rugby got its reward for sticking with a coach they believed would ultimately do the job and land the number one prize in world rugby.

Maybe there is a lesson in that for South African rugby. Between 1997 and 2004, England had one coach. How many did South Africa have? Springbok fans will know the answer themselves: Carel du Plessis, Nick Mallett, Harry Viljoen, Rudolf Straeuli and Jake White. If that doesn't give you a loud and clear message about where the many difficulties in South African rugby lie, then nothing can.

Consistency in the coaching staff leads to consistency in selection. A player gets to know and understand a coach who has been in office that long. The player can prove himself to the coach, win his place in the side, and feel settled and comfortable. Then, chances are, if he is good enough (and presumably he wouldn't have got that far if he wasn't), he can start to concentrate fully on becoming one of the best players in his position in the world. He has no other worries, no distractions. This was the story of England's 2003 World Cup–winning side.

By contrast, there was the Rudolf Straeuli policy of never letting any player feel settled, established and comfortable in the Springbok side, for fear of him starting to believe that he had secured the berth. But what's wrong with that? Didn't Jonny Wilkinson believe he'd secured the England No. 10 jersey long before the World Cup? Didn't Will Greenwood and Mike Tindall feel fairly certain that they'd nailed down the two centre positions? And they played with confidence, poise and self-belief when it came to the highest stage of all, the World Cup.

South African rugby has to learn lessons from all of this, if it is to continue making progress in the future. Ultimately, I think you have to say, Rudolf Straeuli's career as South African rugby coach was dismantled by his own philosophy: never allowing the players to feel comfortable within the team, and never letting them off the leash, allowing them to think and make decisions for themselves. That, as far as I'm concerned, is not the way to handle grown men who will have to make their own decisions on the field of play under the pressures of a major World Cup match.

Teams only achieve the ultimate if they are settled, confident in their own ability and the ability of all those around them, and in that I include the management and coaching staff. In professional rugby union, these things go hand in hand. Settled teams win tournaments, not sides ravaged by dissent, where players fear one bad game might cost them their place. If there is one lesson that came out of the 2003 World Cup for South Africa, it is surely that.

Stability is the first key requirement for a winning team. Until you have that, you have no kind of a platform whatever on which to build the success a team desires.

9
The Rainbow Dream

Transformation and racism have been contentious issues in South African sport – and in South African rugby in particular – since before the country's first democratic election. The process of integration and transformation is perfectly understandable and justified, given the years of exclusion of black and coloured athletes under apartheid. As Nelson Mandela has said, if South Africa is to move forward as a unified country, as it must, equal opportunities should be available to all.

That is the theory, and highly commendable it is. But the trouble has been its implementation. The fact remains that, after more than forty years of apartheid, a huge disparity had arisen between the sporting standards of black and white. That much was inevitable. But how best to address the problem and close the gap? It is a question many South Africans have disagreed on.

Young sportsmen who have been denied access to proper training and facilities are often not ready to be selected to the top teams, and may fail if exposed to first-class rugby when they are not ready for it. Exposure to the very highest levels of any sport, whether it be rugby, cricket, athletics or any other, could prove counterproductive if the young sportsman or woman is not physically and mentally prepared for the challenge.

Already we have seen examples of this in most major sports within South Africa. Without the slightest racist element attached to this view, I think it is unfair to push young people through who might need more time to attain the standards they will be challenged with at the top of their discipline for the benefit of politicians who have their own political agendas.

Young sportspeople should not be used as political pawns. If a player is not good enough for selection to a top team – yet – he or she should be afforded the chance to improve through proper training under the watchful eyes of professional coaches. It all has to begin with selection. Those in charge of choosing sports teams must be as certain as they can possibly be that the players they choose for their team are capable of making the leap to the next level.

I feel great sympathy for those young men from previously disadvantaged backgrounds who were thrust too early into the tough world of international rugby. We have seen several examples in the Springbok rugby team since the first half of the 1990s, when the barriers came down.

Again, I want to stress that I am one hundred per cent for integration. Equal opportunities for all must be created, and the transformation process must move forward until all barriers are removed. If we are to build a great new South Africa and champion sportsmen and women, then we must embrace these principles wholeheartedly.

But that does not mean we have to agree with the rules laid down by politicians, who may be promoting certain issues more for their own benefit than for the young people whom they are supposed to represent. Pushing a young black player into the Springbok team before he is ready or has had the chance to understand the game at the top level, and, more importantly, to adapt to the requirements over a period of time, is not only counterproductive, but will eventually work against him in the long term.

Young black sportsmen who are fast-tracked to the top often find they're just not up to the job. Reaching the peak of your game takes a long time, and not everyone is given sufficient time to develop. It is about more than just being given the opportunity to play at the top level. It is about building longevity and excellence in our rugby players.

A young player who is fast-tracked may play for the Springboks, but the realisation that he can't handle that level of rugby, and that his colleagues are aware that he isn't good enough, is devastating and demoralising. This is a scenario in which everyone loses: the player, his teammates, his team, his family, his friends and his people.

Those who follow South African rugby are well aware of those who have had their chance at the top but have been found wanting. It would be unfair to name those players here, as the blame lies not with them, but with the system. I can only imagine how disappointed they must feel that they could not make their mark at the highest level. Crushing people's dreams and ambitions by prematurely exposing them to the high standards demanded is not the way it should be done.

There are tournaments, such as the Super 12, in which a player has the opportunity to show whether he has got what it takes to succeed once he is given the chance to step up. This is a forum in which he can prove his worth and show his skills over time. If he can handle Super 12 level, it is likely he will be able to step up to international level, as Super 12 rugby contains all the internationals from the three top southern hemisphere countries. There are some very good players in this competition. You will have to be a high-class operator just to survive, never mind stand out. Even so, test rugby is another significant step up even from that.

Too often we've had a scenario where a player is given a few games at provincial or Super 12 level, and then pressure is applied from above on the Springbok coach to select the player for the Boks when he isn't ready. The result has often been disastrous, particularly for the development of the player.

It seems to me that this goes to the very heart of the transformation issue within South African sport. Recently, Archbishop Desmond Tutu called for the abandonment of quotas in South African sports teams, claiming the system was flawed and had been devalued. I share his view completely. I believe that we must give *all* young South Africans the opportunity to excel at the highest level, without excluding anyone on the basis of colour.

The whole tenet of Nelson Mandela's reasoning when he came out of prison was that this should be one country, one nation, as he called it. The country should provide opportunities for all people, regardless of their race or colour. But with quotas, is there not a danger of denying some highly talented young white players their place in a team because room must be found for a specified number of black players? I dislike that idea as much as I dislike the idea of excluding players from previously disadvantaged backgrounds. We should not forget the white element in future South African rugby sides, because they have much to offer. There are many potentially talented white players who live in the country, for example, who might need funds and facilities to break through.

One area where a huge amount of work needs to be done – and Archbishop Tutu spoke out strongly on this – is developing facilities for black or coloured players in disadvantaged areas. Without the proper facilities, a sportsperson cannot improve. In the modern professional game, rugby players need the most advanced technical resources to develop in a physical sense. Other sports demand the same. Gym work, being tested regularly for conditioning and being advised on nutrition – these are all essential aspects in helping a player to reach the peak of their game. You cannot survive at the pinnacle of the game on brute strength or natural ability alone. Although of course both are important, there are many other factors required to reach the top.

One only has to look at the success of the Under 19 and Under 21 South African rugby teams to see the exciting future of rugby in this country. Both teams became world champions at their levels in 2005, beating the best in the world: Australia, New Zealand, France and England. It hardly requires a genius to see that, in the coming years, Springbok rugby teams are going to be completely integrated, perhaps with more players from previously disadvantaged backgrounds than whites. These guys are hugely exciting young rugby players. They have strength, speed, skill and ambition.

I was very excited watching the Under 21s beat Australia to win their tournament in June this year. They had some great athletes, players of real class and promise. But if quotas are to remain in our sport, it seems to me there is a risk that some of these lads might be pushed into the senior Springbok team before their time, just to make up numbers. No one seems to know exactly what those numbers are, but they remain very much a part of the present Springbok rugby set-up. And I find that worrying.

The rush to make places available for these young rugby players is perhaps understandable, as they were denied any opportunity to progress for so long. But I believe in the growing maturity of South Africa as a nation, and I think that sports officials must reflect the progress in our society in their handling of this delicate situation.

No one knows more about patience than Nelson Mandela, and he showed it in abundance when he refused to tolerate any talk of revenge after his release. Instead, he talked of building a new nation where everyone is equal and, in the fifteen years since his release, much has been accomplished. But one factor has been vital: patience. Madiba knew that it would be impossible to make up the forty or more lost years of apartheid in a single decade. It could not happen, no matter how much people may have wanted that to be the case.

But although a lot has been done, patience has been key, and must now be shown by those who administer the sport in this country. Insisting on certain numbers in a team in order to satisfy someone's impatience will surely do more harm than good. Transformation is, after all, steadily moving forward anyway. The promise and talent of the Under 19 and Under 21 lads are such that they are bound to break into future Springbok rugby sides. The only question is when. There are going to be many more Breyton Paulses, Bryan Habanas and Ashwin Willemses. They represent our future as a rugby nation and, personally, I am delighted to see guys like Habana go and play in Pretoria for the Blue Bulls and do so well. His teammates respect his skills and obvious class, and both he and his teammates know he isn't there just as a token of the quota system.

Bryan has achieved his status on merit, and that is the way it should be. He has captured the hearts of all South Africans, whatever their race, colour or background. I love that. I think it is fantastic, not just for him and for the present, but for the future of this country.

No one is going to deny these up-and-coming players of colour their place on merit, because those times have gone for good. They will not be political pawns, or so-called proof that the development of the game among black people is working.

Millions of rands are being spent on coaching in black townships and handing out free T-shirts. But is that the best way forward? Perhaps certain administrators have spent too much time focusing on their own agendas instead of looking after the interests of the people. Use the money to build facilities in black townships so that rugby can really be encouraged in those areas. Giving out piles of T-shirts will not address the underlying problem, which is a lack of resources.

But one thing is certain. Fast-forward ten or twenty years, and the Springbok rugby team will have a very different look to it. The Boks will be a completely integrated team consisting of the best players from every community within this country. I find that wonderfully exciting and positive, a marvellous scenario to anticipate. And it will surely make South Africa potentially one of the strongest rugby nations on earth.

When Jake White took over as Springbok coach in early 2004, he talked of his excitement at the huge talent pool that existed, ready to emerge and strengthen Springbok rugby. He was referring to the increasing numbers of players from previously disadvantaged backgrounds, so that future Springbok teams would be selected from the best, the cream of every community in our country.

Jake isn't alone in feeling a sense of excitement. I do too, and I'm sure that the vast majority of people in this land feel the same way. It's a future scenario to welcome – but not to rush.

And we have to move past the kind of incidents that have so tarnished the good name of South African rugby in the past. Much has been said and written about the alleged racial incident that occurred at the Springbok training camp shortly before the 2003 World Cup. It involved Geo Cronjé, the Blue Bulls forward, and Quinton Davids from Western Province. It became a cause célèbre in South Africa at the time, a shocking indictment on the attitudes of some South African rugby players and South African people.

When I look back, I still find the events that unfolded surreal. We first became aware of a problem when Quinton Davids failed to arrive for an early morning workout session at the training ground. The forwards were due to be out between 6 and 7 a.m., and the backs between 7 and 8 a.m. Quinton didn't pitch at six, but only turned up at seven. Management had given strict instructions that players were not to swap rooms. Quinton had been Geo's roommate, and Geo had arrived at training on time. It soon emerged that Geo had swapped rooms – he didn't want to share with Quinton.

When Quinton turned up late, Joost van der Westhuizen had a go at him, telling him, 'Don't bring your Western Province manners here.' Joost could be like that sometimes. Maybe that was why Ashwin Willemse spoke out against him during Kamp Staaldraad.

When Rudolf Straeuli found out soon afterwards that Geo had refused to share a room with Quinton, he called me over later that afternoon and said that he was going to punish Geo and Quinton for what had happened the night before. He gave me a short account of what had occurred between them. I was appalled. Apparently, Geo had said words to the effect that he was not prepared to share a room or a toilet with a black man.

Their punishment was to run up and down a gravel hill, which ran right around the rugby training ground. As I had an injury and couldn't participate in a contact session with the other players, I chose to join Geo and Quinton. We had to sprint up the hill to the trees at the top, run around the tree and down again, and repeat the exercise right around the perimeter of the field. There must have been over fifty trees around the park, and they were spaced out every five to ten metres. It was exhausting, and Quinton, who wasn't in the best physical shape, really suffered. I had done the exercise before for fitness work and found it tough. Robbie Kempson, who also couldn't do contact work at that time, joined us. We made fifty sprints up that incline, jogged back down and then sprinted back up beside the next tree. No rest was allowed. We did that course three times that afternoon.

Quinton suddenly collapsed from fatigue halfway through the exercise. Geo Cronjé completed the course, but Straeuli told him that what he had done was unacceptable. He told Geo to move back into the room with Quinton. Geo nodded, and I thought that was the end of it. But later, we heard that Geo had again walked out of the room.

I could sense a growing dissatisfaction among the guys in the squad, and decided to call a meeting with all the black players. I said, 'I hear there is unhappiness because Geo has shown no respect by moving out [of the room he shared with Quinton].'

The guys thought he was blatantly showing them that he was a racist, not even bothering to hide it. They were very upset.

Quinton then came up to me and asked us to arrange a contact session so that, in his words, he could 'really f*** up Geo'. If I hadn't realised before how serious the situation was, I certainly did then. Quinton was extremely upset.

I went to see Rudi and told him that, according to Quinton, Geo was still refusing to move back into the room. Straeuli was clear on the matter.

'We will tell him that he either moves back in,' Rudi said, 'or he is out of the World Cup squad.' I agreed with him.

At about the same time, another crisis occurred. Robbie Kempson had decided to withdraw from the squad because of an injury. But there was more to it than met the eye. I was given information that he didn't want to go to the World Cup under Straeuli because he didn't get on with him. One medical report said Robbie could postpone an operation on his elbow until after the World Cup, but Robbie said he didn't want to wait; he wanted it done. I tried to persuade him to stay on, because I'd had a similar injury and played through it until it was convenient to have it fixed. But I couldn't change his mind. Robbie clearly wanted out. So that was that.

But the Geo Cronjé/Quinton Davids incident was to rumble on a lot longer than the Kempson affair. It ended, on the face of it, when Geo telephoned his father and asked him what to do. Apparently, his father, who had also played rugby, told him it was all right, because he'd also had to share toilets in the past with black players. But then the affair became the subject of an official SARFU inquiry.

Two Blue Bulls players approached me for advice, because they were concerned that they might have to testify under oath. Geo had told them why he didn't want to room with Quinton.

SARFU's lawyers questioned me endlessly about the incident. It became obvious that they wanted me to say, 'Yes, Geo is a racist.' But doing that would have shattered Geo's rugby career if they subsequently found him guilty of racial misconduct. I wasn't prepared to be a party to that. So I gave them the facts instead of my opinion. All they needed to do was make up their own minds, but the truth was, they were too soft. The inquiry would eventually find no proof of racial misconduct on Geo's part. I thought it was a weak ruling. Of course no one was going to come out and say Geo was a racist, but from the facts I gave them and the way I phrased my answers, well … If they couldn't make up their minds after that, perhaps they shouldn't have been holding an inquiry in the first place.

As for Geo, I wanted him to learn a lesson that would stand him in good stead in the future. I spoke to Straeuli, and told him I found Geo's attitude unacceptable. Rudi then spoke to Geo, and said that he needed to accept black players and change his attitude, and to lead his life differently. But Geo still did not return to the room he shared with Quinton.

But when Kempson left the camp and was replaced by Schalk Burger, he was put into a room with Quinton, his Western Province teammate. The black guys came to me again and said: 'This is unacceptable, because if Geo is really sorry, he should go straight back in with Quinton.'

They felt that by pairing Schalk with Quinton, Rudi was condoning Geo's actions. I don't believe he was, but that was their opinion. I did, however, agree with them that it was unacceptable that Geo had not moved back. I remember saying to Rudi, 'I think Geo should move back in with Quinton. If he doesn't want to do that, he should go.' In the end, they did move back in together, but only after Rudi had told Geo that he would not be going to the World Cup if he didn't.

Geo and Quinton shared a room for two days, and then the news broke in the press. After that, both were asked to leave the camp.

It was a traumatic time for the squad, and for me as captain. We had to prepare what we were going to say when we heard that the story was going to run in the papers. There was a huge explosion, but I wasn't in the least surprised. The debacle was all over the newspapers, both locally and internationally. It made headlines around the world. Given South Africa's apartheid past, and the way rugby had unified the country during the World Cup in 1995, naturally this was going to be big news. I knew it would put even more pressure on us at the World Cup. And I was right, because when we got to Australia, there were endless questions about the alleged racism in South African rugby. It made me sick to hear this after the players, coach and staff had put in so much hard work.

I think the decision not to let either Geo or Quinton go to the World Cup was flawed. In Geo's case, I agreed that he should not go, because, apart from anything else, he would have been a constant target for anyone trying to pin a racism charge on him during the tournament. It would have been impossible for him to concentrate on rugby with that going on around him. And he would probably have deserved it, because he'd been the cause of so much of the trouble.

But in Quinton's case, the decision to exclude him from the World Cup was totally unacceptable. After all, what had he done wrong? Absolutely nothing. He might have turned up an hour late for a training session, but that did not justify dropping him. Quinton is a good man and he deserved to go to Australia. His situation was handled very badly, and he was very upset about missing the World Cup. I didn't blame him for one minute. Quinton deserved to be in the squad, much more so than a couple of other players I could mention.

I never thought that kind of racial incident would ever happen again in Springbok rugby after 1995. But here it was again, rearing its ugly head. I felt that if a player was a racist, he should have quietly withdrawn from the squad. He could have left for so-called 'personal reasons'. But to make a blatant stand like Geo did was very stupid.

The incident just proved to me that racial integration was something to continually work on in the new South Africa, and indeed within the Springbok team. We had to be aware of prejudice, and the hope that it had been eliminated in 1995 by winning the World Cup was clearly wide of the mark.

In the end, nobody came out of the affair a winner. No one ever does in that type of incident. The black guys in the squad were very upset when Quinton was dropped. I talked to them several times to try to heal the wounds, but it was difficult to judge how they really felt. I will never know whether they were totally honest with me or not.

For me, the incident played a big role in my decision to quit rugby in South Africa. I was tired of dishonesty and having to consort with people I couldn't trust. I'd had enough of it. I wanted to get away from this sort of environment. Of course, the greatest irony of all was that I ran into a similar situation when I got to Northampton!

As for Springbok rugby, I am delighted to say that the next generation of Springbok players will be totally integrated. This generation – my generation, if you like – will soon be gone. We now have youngsters growing up in the new South Africa who are totally integrated in sport and, increasingly, in life. They afford us a wonderful glimpse of an exciting new future. Believe me, when you have been dragged into an affair as deeply unsavoury and disgusting as the Geo Cronjé/Quinton Davids business, you yearn for a future in which such an incident will never happen again.

10
Three Coaches: Mallett, Viljoen and Straeuli

In 1999, I became only the forty-sixth South African ever to captain the Springbok rugby team. It is a fact of which I am very proud, something that will stay with me for the rest of my life.

In the time I played for South Africa, from 1999 to 2003, I worked under three coaches: Nick Mallett, Harry Viljoen and Rudolf Straeuli. In this chapter, I will discuss their very different approaches to rugby coaching, and try to give some insight into three very dissimilar characters.

It is an enduring frustration for me that I missed one small segment of South African rugby history that will forever be remembered with pride and affection. Had I not got injured in 1997, I might well have been involved throughout 1998, the year in which the Boks equalled the world record of seventeen successive test match victories under Nick Mallett. That was one of the best periods in Springbok rugby history.

In fact, I caught the very end of that run, for I was chosen on the bench against England at Twickenham, although I did not get onto the field. But England beat us 13-7 anyway, and our great run was over.

From then on, life got a lot tougher for the Springboks in world rugby. Two factors contributed to this: other rugby-playing countries began to pick up their act and make significant improvements; and several of the key players who had been involved with South Africa for a few years, stretching back to the 1995 World Cup win, such as Gary Teichmann, James Dalton, Krynauw Otto and Mark Andrews, retired from the international game. And we struggled to replace those high-quality players.

The pressure on Nick Mallett suddenly became intense. Of

course, that was typical of South African rugby. Yet here was a man who, in no time at all, had transformed the face of Springbok rugby. He had taken over in September 1997, replacing Carel du Plessis after the shambolic Lions tour, when the Springboks lost the test series 1-2, and taken us to the good times again, winning the Tri-Nations in 1998. Once he took control, an air of confidence that had not been there before permeated the team. He gave the players terrific self-belief because they understood implicitly how he wanted them to play. Mallett set the highest expectations, and that era under him was fantastic for our game. I still regard playing under him as the best part of my career.

But then, as seems to happen so often in South African rugby circles, immediately after a match is lost, the whispers begin. We went down 7-13 at Twickenham, and it was as if all that had gone before now did not count.

The World Cup came and went in 1999 in the northern hemisphere, and South Africa lost, narrowly, to Australia in the semi-finals, but finished third. Yet whatever the outcome, I felt sure that even before the tournament began, the rugby administrators would find a way to get rid of Nick before long. I suppose if we had won the tournament it might have taken them longer to boot him out – but they'd still have done it.

Mallett was in charge of the Boks for thirty-eight internationals and managed to achieve a win ratio of 71 per cent in that time. I think that is as good as it gets – or damn near to it anyway.

They found the stick with which to beat Mallett in Durban before the last Tri-Nations match of 2000. The Springbok coach had mentioned that he thought tickets for the test match (R300) were too expensive. Unbeknownst to Mallett, the person he was speaking to was a journalist, and she wrote the story. That did it. Mallett was eventually called before the SARFU disciplinary tribunal for having criticised the Union in public, allegedly contrary to the terms of his contract. He was told that he no longer

With my hero, Nelson Mandela, and John Smit prior to the 2003 Rugby World Cup

A lighter moment with Rudolf Straeuli at a Brisbane press conference during the World Cup

Congratulating 'Big Joe' van Niekerk on his try against Samoa

Leading the team onto the field for the first-round game against England, Subiaco Oval, Perth

Draped in the South African flag for a World Cup photo shoot

Referee Peter Marshall talking to Martin Johnson and me

Leaving the field with Helen Millson, the WP and Stormers' physio, Ellis Park, February 2004

Neil de Kock, me and Schalk Burger in action against the Brumbies at Newlands, March 2004

Celebrating our 51-23 win over the Blues at Eden Park, Auckland, April 2004

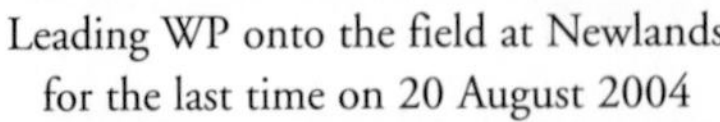

Leading WP onto the field at Newlands
for the last time on 20 August 2004

One of the Newlands faithful

Neil de Kock and I celebrate
my successful drop goal

Carried off the field by David Hendricks and
Adri Badenhorst at the end of my last game for WP

In the changing room
after the game

Playing for Northampton

Shaking hands with Matt Dawson (London Wasps), October 2004

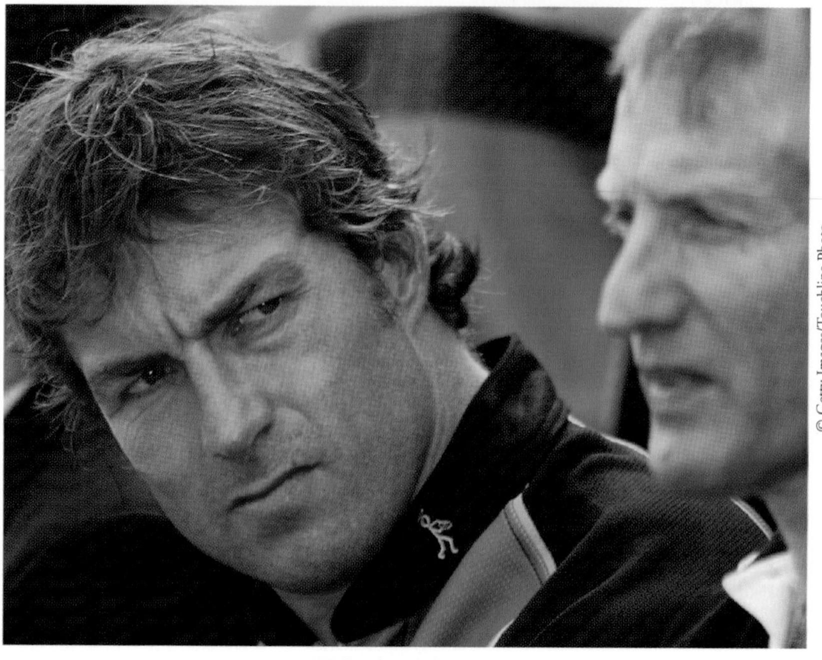

With Alan Solomons at Northampton

Chatting to Carlos Spencer during training for the Jonah Lomu–Martin Johnson Testimonial game, June 2004

Captaining a winning side at Twickenham at last! With the Tibco Challenge Trophy as captain of the Barbarians against England, May 2005

Full circle: returning to Paarl Boys' High with some members of the Springbok team to play a game of touch rugby

With Justine and baby Sophia at home in Cape Town, 2005

had the support of the Union, and a severance package was negotiated. Just as the Springboks were due to take off for their end-of-year tour to Argentina and the northern hemisphere in late October 2000, Mallett was gone. As far as I was concerned, South African rugby was the chief loser.

I still wonder to this day what went on in the minds of those who controlled South African rugby at the time. Did they just not like Mallett any more? Were they jealous of his achievements? Did they resent someone else hogging most of the headlines? Or were the men who ran SARFU tired of the high standards Mallett set for them? Mallett was a professional – he expected everyone, from players to administrators, to give their best.

Whatever the real reasons for Mallett's sacking, I still regret the way he was dispensed with, and how much our rugby lost as a result of that crazy decision.

Mallett was a coach who always put the players first. He made sure that they got whatever they wanted. He believed in laying the basic foundations for players to perform, and then giving them the responsibility to act, to produce as close to their best as possible.

Of course, Nick was outspoken on any subject, the authorities included, and this trait tended to go down like a lead balloon at management level. It is my experience that the one thing rugby authorities do not like – and this applies right around the world – is criticism. They seem to believe they are above censure and that no one should question them. But Nick said what he thought, and of course that made him enemies. In the end, I think they were just tired of him. He had given them so much grief, they just wanted to be rid of him.

But the thought of putting South African rugby first didn't seem to occur to the rugby bosses. If Mallett was still the best man for the job – and if you'd asked the players, they would have given him a ringing endorsement – then surely he should have stayed. At what point do those in authority decide to put the well-being of the game second to their own personal preferences? Because that is exactly what happened when they got rid of Nick.

All players know when a good coach comes along, and Nick Mallett certainly was one. He was one of the most liked and respected rugby coaches South Africa has ever had. In fact, for South Africa to have produced Kitch Christie, who steered the 1995 squad to the World Cup, and, not long after, Nick Mallett, says a lot about the rugby knowledge and coaching ability in this country.

Nick was respected not because he was a disciplinarian (although he was), but because he knew what he was doing; he was a damn good coach.

After he left the job, several people asked me whether I thought there was a finite period for a rugby coach in office. My answer was, yes, there is truth in that. But as regards Nick, he left far too early. Even if he had been asked to step down as national coach, he would have made a superb job of coaching other coaches in South Africa, a role that would have been beneficial for all South African rugby. In 2004 and 2005, we saw some of Nick Mallett's influence in some of Jake White's work as Springbok coach. Jake had worked under Nick as technical adviser in the Bok set-up during the time they equalled the world record of seventeen test victories, and he must have learnt a huge amount from him.

Certainly, what Nick didn't know about coaching wasn't worth knowing. His passion for rugby and his deep-seated knowledge of the game were qualities you could not easily replace. But – and it has happened far too much in recent years – someone with a great deal to offer was allowed to be snatched from South African rugby for the benefit of an overseas club.

Nick went to the Paris-based French club Stade Français, and made so outstanding a success of his job that the club won the coveted French national championship (League Nationale de Rugby) two years in a row under him. That just confirmed

Mallett's ability to build a winning side and command respect from his players.

But no human being is perfect and, as I mentioned earlier, Nick began to feel the pressures of the Springbok coaching job. The more the pressure, the more he demanded results from his players, and that put additional pressure on them. In the end, something had to give.

With hindsight, I would say that, apart from alienating the rugby bosses, Nick's biggest mistake was not to take Gary Teichmann to the 1999 World Cup as his captain. I have no idea why he didn't, except to surmise that Gary wasn't his number one choice for the No. 8 jersey. Gary's leadership would have made a big difference. We may not have won the World Cup had Gary been there, but the rugby public bore Nick tremendous resentment for that decision.

But Nick knew what he wanted and made sure he got it. You never approached Nick Mallett unless you knew what you were talking about. If you talked a lot of rubbish to him, he would blow you out of the water.

Nick was a fierce taskmaster. At our video meetings, when the coaches had analysed each player's performance and been through the tapes with them, the guys would be very nervous. You knew that if you'd made a mistake, you were in serious trouble.

And, ironically, Mallett was particularly hard on the players after a win. Then he would take them out on a Monday morning and absolutely annihilate them on the training ground. He knew full well the guys were feeling a bit fragile after a few beers on the weekend. But, conversely, he went easy on players if they'd lost. He knew their confidence had to be rebuilt before the next match. The players really respected him. He had a way of enforcing discipline that never made the guys hate him.

Mind you, André Venter might not have called Nick his favourite guy after he made André stand up in one video session in Australia and gave him an absolute bollocking. The players got a real fright. André didn't enjoy being singled out, and didn't handle it very well. But Nick wanted the players to understand that rugby is a team sport, and if an individual decides to play a game in his own way, you can lose a test match. If a player does not buy into the system and play according to its structures because he likes doing his own thing, it causes problems.

To my knowledge, nobody ever took Nick Mallett on, not unless it was done behind closed doors. Somehow, Mallett managed to find the balance between being popular with players and having their respect, and being a tough taskmaster too. Players knew that if they stepped out of line, they'd get hammered. Nick never left any of us in any doubt whatsoever about that. But after the bollockings at the video sessions, it would be over and forgotten, the lessons digested. You'd be playing golf with him later that day. But that's key in a relationship between coach and player; he has to instil respect, not fear.

When Nick was dumped as national coach, there was huge disappointment and insecurity among the players. I felt lost personally, as he was the only Springbok coach I had known. Others just felt, 'Here we go again. It's back to the bad old ways of South African rugby.'

Nobody knows what the future holds, least of all those who follow (or should that be 'endure'?) the fortunes of South African rugby. But I am pleased that Nick Mallett is now back in South Africa, and involved with Western Province, passing on and using his immense rugby knowledge for the benefit of our game and players. I sincerely hope he will coach South Africa again in the future.

The Australian Bob Dwyer coached the Wallabies on more than one occasion, and the second time he took charge, he led them to their 1991 World Cup triumph. That might be an example worth remembering.

Nick's departure came just as the Springboks were preparing for their tour – hardly an ideal time to make a change. His replacement was quickly named as Harry Viljoen, with Jake White as his assistant coach. Harry was certainly different. A hugely successful businessman, he had made a fortune in the financial planning industry, and now had the financial security for life to take on any job. It was irrelevant whether the position offered the kind of money he was used to, as he had more than enough to last a lifetime.

But Harry wasn't just a businessman; he knew his rugby as well. By the age of nineteen, he'd made his debut as a provincial rugby player in South Africa, and he was a useful scrumhalf for Transvaal in his day. Unlike Mallett, he never played for the Springboks, but he became a coach early in his life (at thirty), steered Transvaal to two Currie Cup finals, moved on to Natal, and also took them to a final. After a bit of a break, he resurfaced at Western Province in 1997, and took us to the Currie Cup title that year when we beat Free State 14-12 in the final at Cape Town.

The following year, Harry coached the Stormers in Super 12, without success. We lost so many matches that he resigned, saying coaching was no longer for him. Imagine everyone's surprise when Harry Viljoen was given the job of Springbok coach after Mallett's sacking!

Harry came in as South Africa's eighth coach in eight years since the country's readmission to the international game in 1992, and did exactly what he had done at Western Province in 1997. He is very good at marketing, very good on screen. He put together a video presentation outlining what he wanted to do with Springbok rugby. He told the players that he required intelligent, business-like rugby players who would use their brains, and be professional both on and off the field. He split South African rugby into a commercial (SA Rugby) and non-commercial (SARFU) arm, so that decisions could be made without red tape. That was his brainchild. He didn't want a lot of regional rugby presidents voting on everything.

I think he had the right idea, because he said, let's run it as a business, and the senior players will be like directors of the board. He had huge player input.

Harry certainly knew what he wanted. A while before, the Springbok team had superb sponsors for its clothing, companies like Polo, Nike and Rockport. We'd get really good-quality stuff. But somewhere along the line these arrangements ended and we finished up with much inferior clothing. Harry came in, looked at this situation and said, 'This is unacceptable. We are not going to wear this stuff. We are going to be highly professional and we're going to wear the best, like Gucci and Armani.' Of course, he had the money to buy anything he wanted, and poor taste in clothing just wasn't Harry Viljoen's style. He wanted the best players in South Africa to look their best. It quickly became apparent that he had the sartorial principles right.

But unfortunately Harry wasn't very good at telling the players what he really thought of them. He couldn't be honest with them, or with his staff. He wouldn't select me in his squad to go overseas in 2001, but handed me the sop of being made captain of the 'A' side. He broke the news through the press two weeks before the tour, which bewildered me. But then Danie Rossouw of the Blue Bulls damaged his shoulder and I was brought into the senior squad. Although I wasn't in the starting line-up, I did get on from the bench against Italy in Genoa and against England at Twickenham. Joe van Niekerk was also on the bench, and it seemed as if Harry was just using us as impact players, no more than that.

The problem was, Harry's teams were losing test matches. We'd only just scraped home 37-33 against Argentina in Buenos Aires in the first match of our end-of-season tour that year, which was also Harry's first test in charge. We did beat Ireland and Wales on that tour, but then went down 17-25 at Twickenham.

On the morning before the England game, Harry asked me to have breakfast with him. By then, I had increasingly felt him to be a weak man; he could never look you in the eye. He wouldn't say, 'Look, this is what I want you to do to improve, and if you can't do it you won't be in my team.' Instead he preferred to skirt around the issue. Harry just couldn't be direct. Confrontation was not his style.

Yet he said to me that morning, and I've never forgotten his words, 'You are my number one flanker. You are part of the process and I will bring you through at the right time.' The trouble was, all Harry's actions up to that time had told me I wasn't seriously in his plans at all. So I thought to myself, 'If I was a kid I'd probably believe you.' But I took it all with a big pinch of salt.

Harry didn't understand that the coach has to take responsibility and talk to the players. The coach must sit down with the guys, even individually at times, look them squarely in the eye and put them in the picture. It is a tough but necessary part of the process. But Harry wasn't strong enough to do that. He was always trying to avoid confrontational situations, and the players never knew where they stood. As a result, he never really gained the players' confidence and respect, and there was general unhappiness in the Springbok squad. I remember at one point, about ten members of the squad were considering leaving the country, to take up offers from clubs overseas. I was one of them.

After the tour of the UK ended in late 2001 with a match against the Barbarians, I stayed on for a few days to go down to the West Country to visit Bath rugby club. They had contacted my agent, and it looked as if I would end up there. The town is a delight, the club had a great reputation and tradition, and it seemed the right move for me. I was frustrated and fed up with rugby in South Africa and sick of trying, without success, to get back into the Springbok side as a first choice. I couldn't see any future for me with the Boks as long as Harry Viljoen remained coach. I found that, like so many others, I never knew where I stood with him.

Harry was also very indecisive about selection. On one occasion, when he was due to announce the Springbok team, he couldn't make up his mind who to play at scrumhalf. He kept delaying the live announcement on M-Net. Harry's choice was between Neil de Kock from WP and Deon de Kock from the Falcons. Although Harry had played Neil de Kock more regularly, to everyone's surprise he suddenly selected Deon de Kock. People thought it was Neil's name that appeared on TV, and congratulated him, but it turned out to be the other De Kock. The same thing happened to Toks van der Linde. His name appeared on the press release and was then removed. Rumour has it that Harry changed the names as they were released to the media.

His work in fitness matters also did not impress me. He and his assistants would run the players into the ground, but I always had the feeling it came from a book. There was no planning to it, no structure. Worse still, the players soon realised that the coach seemed more interested in shopping than rugby. On several occasions during the tour of the UK, Harry would return to the hotel in the afternoon, laden with bags bearing labels such as 'Armani', 'Gucci', 'Eden Park' or whatever. We wondered where he found the time to tour the shops when he was supposed to be in charge of a rugby tour, planning test matches and strategies, supposedly dealing with players. Of course, there would be coaching sessions, but in between he seemed to spend a lot of time shopping. We didn't feel Harry had his mind totally on the job. Financially, he didn't need it, and a lot of us wondered why he had taken it on. It didn't seem to make any sense.

South African rugby coaches have to coach at the top levels of the game in order to make serious money and set themselves up financially. But that never applied to Harry. We came to the conclusion that the position must have appealed to his ego.

Yes, some of the players liked Harry Viljoen as a person and certainly admired him for what he had done in the business world, where he had obviously been brilliant. He'd made so much money that, around the time he was appointed Springbok coach, he flew first class to Australia, at his own expense, to talk rugby and exchange ideas about the game and its tactics with the Aussie coaches Bob Dwyer and Rod Macqueen. Not everyone can afford to do that.

And he had some good ideas, because he brought in experts in several fields, people such as Les Kiss, a defensive coach with a background in Rugby League, Frank Ponissi, also a defensive coach, and kicking guru Michael Byrne. Harry was always trying to pick other people's brains to extend his own knowledge. Unfortunately, he got it into his mind that we had to play the game like the Wallabies in order to be successful. He believed it was a certain route to success to follow their lead, because of their 1999 World Cup win. But the fact is, Australia could play the game they did because they had George Gregan and Stephen Larkham. It was as simple as that. There was no way we could play the same game as Australia. I believe Viljoen should've approached it from a different angle: look at the players you have available and what style they can play, and try to build around that. You can't play a multi-phased game when half the guys aren't capable of it. But Harry just wanted to copy the Australians. And of course, what Harry couldn't see was that the Australians were more than happy to offer him this information, because they knew the Springboks would never beat them at their own game. We traditionally play a different type of rugby; it is physical and a huge pressure game, whereas the Australians hold the ball through many phases. In recent years, they have outsmarted a lot of teams just because of the Gregan/Larkham pairing at halfback. We had other halfbacks with other strengths. But they wouldn't fit into an Australian game plan.

Harry's overall view was that if we did better and better in terms of results, there would be more money for everyone. But Harry missed the vital ingredient, which was that all we wanted was a strong, honest coach who would put us in the picture, be frank and upfront with us, and whom we could respect. But unfortunately, we didn't have that.

Harry had changed since his days as Western Province and Stormers coach. In 1997, I was always Harry's first-choice flanker, and I thought that after that season he appreciated what I could bring to the team. But of course, it isn't just about strengths: a coach must know all sides of his players, both their strengths and weaknesses. He must also understand their make-up, what kind of a person they are. For instance, some players react well to a good old-fashioned bollocking, others turn inwards and it is the worst thing to do to them if you want to restore their confidence. A coach's job is not just about team tactics and choosing the starting XV; he must be aware of what makes his players tick, how they will react in given situations, what can inspire them, what things to avoid when dealing with them. The best coaches find out all these things about their players so that they get the absolute best out of them. Those who don't are less successful.

But between 1997 and 2000, Harry had clearly changed his mind about me. He didn't seem to like me any more. Either that, or he had a certain idea of how he wanted his team to play and I didn't fit into the game plan. Mind you, it was some idea.

Harry became obsessed with the idea that the Springboks ought to throw the ball around the whole field. It didn't seem to matter to him that, traditionally, we have played a much closer type of game, utilising the natural strength of our big forwards and playing tighter rugby. But suddenly, all that was bunkum, history. Harry wanted to see us running around the field, no arguments. So much so, in fact, that he picked Percy Montgomery at fly half, and when the Boks went to Buenos Aires to play Argentina in November 2000, he gave firm instructions that we should not kick the ball at all.

Now that is extremely difficult to do if you are trying to win a test match. There are bound to be times in a game when you have to kick, when it is not only sensible to kick from a defensive point of view, but also shrewd to kick in an attacking sense. But Harry wasn't prepared to see anyone kick the ball, so we ended up in a kind of harum-scarum type of game, which ended 37-33 in the Boks' favour. A few senior players watched this happening and privately shook their heads in dismay. They knew it couldn't work, that this type of game had only a limited shelf life.

Harry wanted big guys in the back row. He picked them ahead of me. So, in one test, we had a combination of André Vos, André Venter and Bobby Skinstad. That meant we didn't have a genuine open-side flanker. All were fine players, of course, no doubt about it. But every team needs a breakaway, a guy used to winning the ball on the ground and operating at speed.

But in the end, even guys like Vos tired of Harry and his tactics. At the start of 2002, André, who had been South Africa's Player of the Year for 2001, quit South African rugby to fly to London and join the Harlequins club. He was a huge loss to our game, because he could have had several more years at the top level.

Around the same time that Vos quit, Mark Andrews finished, and then Percy Montgomery went to Wales. Pieter Rossouw and Robbie Kempson also left. Marius Hurter had been with the English club Newcastle for some seasons already by that time. Players were deserting South African rugby, and I'd have joined them had I not heard via the grapevine that Harry's days might be numbered.

People outside South African rugby don't understand that although it's great to play for the Springboks, there is nothing worse than losing games and not enjoying yourself. If you are not in an environment where you can perform, where you are encouraged to be yourself, to go out and perform on the rugby field, then there isn't any pleasure in it any more.

With Harry Viljoen, one always felt that one had to be careful how one behaved off the field as well. He would take off-the-field behaviour into consideration when he chose his teams. And he would make up his mind about you by the way you dressed and handled yourself in the week. That makes players think they have to watch their every move. They can no longer relax. And while I approve of high standards for Springbok players off the field, I do not believe players will produce their best if they are constantly on edge, worried about saying or doing the wrong thing, or not appearing to fit the bill in some way. Under Harry's reign as Springbok coach, you couldn't be the person you truly were. He didn't actually say that, but I knew this was the case.

In all, Harry Viljoen was coach of South Africa for around eighteen months, and it was not a successful period. We finished bottom of the Tri-Nations table each year and lost too many of our major test matches. Towards the end of 2001, the Boks had lost 15-26 to New Zealand in Auckland, and 10-20 to France in Paris. At one stage, we were even making hard work of overcoming Italy in Genoa (54-26). Then we lost 9-29 to England at Twickenham. The writing was on the wall.

But the other side to Viljoen's era was that it seriously messed up the lives and careers of people like the Australian backs coach Tim Lane, whom Harry had brought in as his assistant. Tim had been backs coach with the Wallabies when they won the 1999 World Cup, and Harry clearly thought he could play a major role through his experience of Australian rugby, which Harry always wanted us to move towards. But it didn't work out.

No one ever considers the personal sacrifices these arrangements demand. Tim took his kids out of school and moved his whole family from Sydney to South Africa. He bought into the scheme and tried to play his part, even though it was doomed to fail. In January 2002, when things got tough and the results were not forthcoming, Harry just walked away, leaving Tim in the lurch. I had long expected that Harry would 'bomb'. There was only ever a remote chance that he could convince the guys to buy into his marketing plans and the way he wanted to run the team. But he had 'bombed' before under pressure, at the Stormers, when they did very badly in the Super 12. Now he was doing it again.

Harry's public parting shot was that 'The media are unrelenting in South Africa. Frankly, I could not deal with the constant negatives.' He should have tried being a soccer manager in England with the British tabloid newspapers to assassinate him every morning. Now that must be *real* pressure.

I confess I could never really 'place' Harry Viljoen. Certainly I never knew where I stood with him. On a personal level, he was friendly and generous. He surrounded himself with knowledgeable people, and didn't mind sharing his wealth. People told me he could be very generous. And that is a good business principle: finding good people and getting them on board.

Also, when it came to things like PowerPoint presentations, visuals that would excite people and make them want to get involved, he was terrific. That was his business genius coming out. And all he needed to do was back that up with the personal touch. But he never did that, and it surprised me. Another problem was that he didn't really have deep-seated rugby knowledge, probably because he had been out of the game for some time when he was appointed. With hindsight, it wasn't the right role for him. If you'd wanted a top-notch businessman who could help you become hugely successful in terms of organisational structure, Harry would have been your man. His record spoke for itself; frankly, it was almost second to none. But other skills are required to run rugby teams, and some of them Harry just didn't possess. It was a shame, really.

So, on 1 March 2002, Rudolf Straeuli was appointed to replace Harry Viljoen as Springbok coach. And generally his appointment was perceived as a positive, for Rudi was a man who knew rugby football down to his boots. He had been a part of the famous 1995 Rugby World Cup–winning squad, and was one of the heroes of Springbok rugby. He had spent all his life in rugby in some capacity, and, as well as that, had coached Natal to success, and also had experience of coaching in England. Rugby supporters, particularly those up north and in KwaZulu-Natal, didn't think he could go wrong.

I knew Rudi well from playing the two Currie Cup finals

against Natal in 2000 and 2001, and also playing against him once in a trial match after the 1995 World Cup. He was a big, strong competitor.

The word was, the national selectors had only asked for South Africans to apply for the job. A shortlist of four was reputedly drawn up: Rudi Joubert, Alistair Coetzee, Jake White and Straeuli. I'd heard a whisper that Nick Mallett could be up for it, but whether that was true, I don't know. I also heard that Gert Smal had applied, but that he'd found out via the grapevine that Straeuli was favoured, and withdrew his application. There is always rumour and intrigue when a Springbok coach is about to be appointed. At times, it's like the cardinals selecting a new pope. Only when you see the white smoke do you know a final choice has been made.

There wasn't white smoke in this case, but there was a strong, powerfully built, traditional rugby man who was introduced to the press as South African rugby's new saviour. And one look at Rudolf Straeuli told you that he wouldn't be touring the shops in London and returning to the team hotel carrying bags with designer clothes. Not Rudi.

I was just pleased to see Harry depart. I wanted to give it another go with the Boks, and I hoped I'd get a fair crack of the whip with Straeuli. I didn't actually care who got the job; I just wanted the opportunity to prove myself again.

Rudi started very well; he had the right ideas. He wanted to go back to the basics of South African rugby. He wasn't interested in borrowing a style from another country, but preferred to play to our traditional strengths. He knew how potent a cocktail that could be; after all, he had been a member of the World Cup–winning squad that had beaten strong rugby nations like France, Australia and New Zealand. Yet he surprised a lot of people with his early test selections, picking players such as Brent Russell, Bolla Conradie, André Pretorius and Joe van Niekerk, young guys of unbelievable talent.

They came in and did very well for him, because in the 2002 Tri-Nations, we scored more tries than either Australia or New Zealand. Alas, we still ended up last on the log, as we also conceded the most tries: sixteen, compared to ten by Australia and only six by the All Blacks, who won the competition.

Straeuli brought back trials, a move that pleased many rugby fans in South Africa. But I thought it was ridiculous. Asking players to appear in a trial match when they had been playing Super 12 for two months or more was bizarre. What on earth could a coach hope to learn from a single, one-off performance when he could have been studying players in competition against the best players of New Zealand and Australia? It didn't make any sense to me.

Rudi's belief was that some of the top South African players had gone a bit soft. Each year, the Springboks had held a training camp, based at a luxury hotel in Plettenberg Bay. Rudi wanted to apply a bit of shock treatment, so he cancelled the hotel booking and made arrangements to take the squad to the altogether more basic South African Police Training College in Pretoria. You didn't go there to relax and soak up the sun, but Rudi was determined to do something about what he saw as a 'flawed culture'. We checked into simple bungalows, and I reflected on what it meant to be part of the Springbok rugby squad again.

Besides being part of the team, Rudi had asked me to be his captain. We got on from the word go. I think he enjoyed the way I played and liked me as a person. Both times when Western Province beat his Sharks to land the Currie Cup in 2000 and 2001, we had been quite far behind. I was captain in both matches: perhaps he respected me for that. But perhaps, above all else, he liked Afrikaans people, or someone who was a little more conservative, like me.

I'd heard that SARFU wanted to appoint Bobby Skinstad as captain, and I wouldn't have had a problem with that. I got on very well with Bobby. Basically, we had decided very early on in our careers that we were completely different, and we just accepted each other. We might compete for the captaincy but never for the same position in the team, because we played a different game. We couldn't see any reason why we shouldn't both be selected.

In the end, I heard via the grapevine, as you usually do, that Straeuli preferred me for the job. He called me to a meeting and asked me what I thought about being captain. We both spoke about the need for a relationship based on trust, and he said that would ultimately determine the success or failure of the team.

I asked Rudi just one question. I said, 'Look, to be quite honest, I've heard that SA Rugby, through Rian Oberholzer, want to put pressure on you to select Bobby. Are you going to listen to them?'

He said, 'Yes, it's true, there are people here who don't want you as captain, but I will make that decision.'

I appreciated his honesty.

So Rudi had the job, and he soon gave me the captaincy. It was a tremendous privilege. And I always gave my utmost, all I had, to make a success of it.

One thing I quickly came to understand about Rudolf Straeuli, although not all the Springbok players of that time will agree with me, was that he was honest in what he tried to achieve. The mistakes he made – and he certainly made plenty – were at least genuine mistakes.

It started off well enough. We won our first four games of 2002, twice beating Wales, then Argentina and Samoa. But the nagging doubts at the back of people's minds that these straightforward, almost regulation victories over weaker opposition were not ideal preparation for the tough stuff that would follow – New Zealand in Wellington, Australia in Brisbane and New Zealand in Durban – were proved accurate. We lost all three matches. We did beat Australia 33-31 in a thrilling return Tri-Nations match in Johannesburg, thanks to a try and conversion from our fullback Werner Greeff in added time after the hooter had sounded. But we then embarked upon a nightmare tour of the northern hemisphere, where we lost all three tests, to France, Scotland and England. It was a real roller-coaster ride of a year, culminating in the disastrous Twickenham debacle.

And, like all Springbok coaches before him, and doubtless like all those who will follow, Rudi went through a rough time as results started to go against him. Worse still, he started getting paranoid, especially about discipline. I believe his security consultant, Adriaan Heijns, contributed to his mindset. Rudi began to use him to spy on the players to see what time they came in, little things like that. And that was one of the problems that would just escalate. He didn't trust the players enough, and he wasn't prepared to treat them like adults and allow them to make their own decisions on matters such as discipline.

Sure, if a guy comes in at three in the morning when he's supposed to be preparing for a test match, you throw the book at him and your confidence in the entire squad is bound to be shaken. Any coach is entitled to expect something better from a senior group of professional rugby players. But, to my knowledge, that sort of thing wasn't happening regularly, and certainly not close to test matches. If it was, I certainly wasn't aware of it.

Far from allowing a flexible working relationship in which all parties could breathe freely, in which players could air their opinions and raise questions, Rudi tended to hammer anyone who challenged him.

I want to state unequivocally that, when I look back, I realise I made a major mistake because I did not challenge him enough, which I regret. The problem was, Rudi got rid of a lot of the senior players who would have stood up to him. Robbie Kempson didn't want to play under him, and he wasn't the only one. Rudi allegedly told Robbie Fleck that he would give him his chance, but the only opportunity he was given was against Namibia. Fleck called him a liar, and Rudi didn't like that. It was the end of Fleck as a Springbok. The few players who did challenge him were quickly gone.

AJ Venter told him to his face, 'You work on fear. The guys fear you, and that's wrong.' AJ never played again under Rudolf.

As a group of players in those circumstances, it is much easier to stand together and say, 'Let's go and see the coach and sort this out.' But I had so few senior players around me. Bobby Skinstad, who would have been prepared to do something about it, wasn't there. Joost van der Westhuizen was, and although he was probably the most senior player, he is also a very conservative type of guy, and besides, he approved of some of the things Rudi was doing.

Others didn't, and I knew that. I also knew that I had to say something. I mentioned the players' dissatisfaction to Rudi. They hated his rules, for example having to wear the same colour T-shirts and eating breakfast at the same time. It was all such a waste of time and energy.

'Come and tell me what you think, come and talk to me,' Rudi said, in his avuncular manner. So I thought to myself, tell him. Never turn around and think later that you should have spoken up. So I went to see him, and found it difficult to challenge him on certain things because of the strange way he had of manipulating people. And he manipulated us. He didn't brainwash us, but, looking back, I felt intimidated, and this prevented me from fully airing the players' concerns. I somehow felt it was too dangerous, that he would take it personally. Did I want to say so much that I'd be dropped and perhaps not get back in the team? Although I didn't think I would lose the job that day if I told him everything, I did fear that my honesty might count against me and cost me the job in the long term. I also didn't think he would listen only to me.

I suppose the bottom line is that I wasn't brave enough to state my case. Today, I deeply regret my inability to speak up, because that aspect of my captaincy failed. I let the players down by not standing up to the coach. I always felt I had the respect of the players, and I am sure I did on the field. But, looking back now, and talking to some of those who were around at the time, like AJ Venter, I feel embarrassed at my failings.

Players have a great survival instinct. So much so that they seem to sense when they can't be open and frank with their coach and captain. They fear he might take what they have to say the wrong way. And that's what I feared in this instance.

The trouble was, you never quite knew what Rudi was thinking or planning. When we went to Melbourne for the World Cup quarter-final, we were looking forward to staying at a wonderful hotel on the river, a beautiful place we knew from a previous visit. Spirits were high as we headed out to the hotel, even though we knew we had to meet New Zealand in the quarter-finals.

But we drove straight past it, out of the city centre, and ended up in a place in the middle of nowhere, far out of Melbourne. I got off the bus and said, 'Why are we here?'

Rudi gave a wry smile and said he thought this was 'better' for us. I knew at once it had been his decision. He didn't want us to be right in the middle of the city, next to the shops and other distractions. He didn't trust us in that environment. But that was rubbish, and it was also counterproductive. A lot of the players were disappointed in the new place, and you could see how the shoulders slumped.

As players, we wanted to stay in a place that would make us feel good, even spoilt, reminding us how fortunate we were to be at the World Cup, staying in such a lovely hotel. I feel certain it would have lifted us and inspired us for the game. But instead we trudged into our new hotel with dark expressions.

Something similar had happened when we stayed in Durban for test matches under Rudi. Before, we always used to stay at the Beverly Hills Sun Intercontinental, at Umhlanga Rocks, a lovely location and a fantastic hotel overlooking the Indian Ocean. You just felt good to be alive when you woke up there. Everything felt right with the world, and you were inspired to run onto the field and show you were the best player in the world. But when Rudi took over as Bok coach and the subject was brought up about where we would stay in Durban and the Intercontinental was mentioned, Rudi said, 'Oh, that's a holiday place; we're going to work.' So we stayed at another hotel that was much inferior.

Something else that disturbed me was that the players never really confided in me. I never knew what they were thinking or saying behind my back. I assumed it was because the relationship between a coach and his captain is traditionally very close, and they might have thought I wouldn't listen to their views, and that I'd take Rudi's side in an argument. They may have seen me as an extension of him.

It think it all reverts to the fear factor Rudi tried to instil among the players. I always thought that philosophy was nonsense. You don't need to fear a coach to produce your best. I doubt very much that I'll ever be a coach, but if I were, I would encourage the players to be the people they want to be. Let them grow their hair long or grow a beard if that's what they want. And I would put them up in the best hotels, give them the best treatment and let them have access to top facilities. But when they run onto the field, they would have to play; they would have to deliver. There would be no excuses if you have given them the best of everything and they don't perform. If that happened, I would be ruthless.

But at the World Cup under Rudi Straeuli, we weren't allowed any freedom and we weren't given the chance to be individuals. But we didn't really perform either. It was a lose-lose situation. Rudi didn't like the idea of guys growing their hair or not shaving. He wants players to look neat and tidy. Personally, I'd have the scruffiest, most unkempt group of players in the world under my charge if they went on the field and blitzed every opponent. That would be good enough for me.

Rudi would say to us, 'You would shave and cut your hair if

you had an appointment with your bank manager. So why don't you do the same when you come down to breakfast with me, as I decide whether you get a salary or not?' The players responded very negatively to that sort of line.

Nick Mallett got it right in this regard. He would let the players have their way, but if any of them ever gave the slightest impression that they were bigger than the team, then he would smash them.

Rudi's approach was to treat the players like children, distrusting their ability to be sensible and make decisions when they were left to their own devices. But how on earth can you then expect them to make decisions when they get on a rugby field?

The coach must prepare his charges as best he possibly can, but he also has to leave scope for individualism. Otherwise, how can a player make a vital decision in an instant during a game, how can he size up an opportunity or choose the right moment to exploit a gap? He has to be used to thinking for himself and making his own decisions. If he isn't, he will go out as some kind of pre-programmed robotic figure who simply follows his coach's instructions to the last letter. And if a glorious opportunity arises before him to make a break or do something that is not in the script, he will spurn it, because it isn't in the coach's game plan. If almost all the decision-making processes of individual players are taken over by the coach in preparation, then he cannot expect his players to go on the field and suddenly start making brilliant, visionary decisions. He can't have it both ways.

So, on reflection, I am critical of the decisions Rudi made when the pressure was on. In his favour, I would make the point equally forcefully that no one understands the real pressures of being Springbok coach, especially at a World Cup. The expectations are enormous, probably far above the reach of most human beings. We expect – no, *demand* is a better word – the impossible from the Springbok coach. He must not only win the tournament (and 1995 will be a millstone around our necks at every World

Cup until we win it again), but also produce fantastic rugby to satisfy the demanding South African rugby fans.

Everyone in South Africa believes they could do a better job than the incumbent coach, and they're not afraid to say so. They think it's a cinch to select a Springbok side, especially from the comforts of their couch. Winning or losing doesn't affect the armchair expert. But when your whole life – your family, your salary, your future – depends on whom you select, those clear-cut decisions are suddenly not so clear-cut any more.

While it is great to have the support of the fans and their devotion to the game, we should remember that all that microscopic attention translates into a fearsome pressure on the coach. He is expected to deliver the goods – the trophy – and he knows from the day he starts that anything less than that just will not be good enough. It is a task that is, quite honestly, beyond the powers of most human beings. Indeed, perhaps it is significant that no country has ever won the Rugby World Cup and retained it. And I don't think it will happen in France in 2007 either. That reveals something of the pressures involved in the World Cup, and the man standing right in the firing line is the coach.

In South Africa, the Springbok rugby coach is under the same intensity of expectation every time the team plays, not just at a World Cup. Any criticism therefore has to be balanced by these factors.

But, having said that, I had been very positive about Rudi as Springbok coach when he began. He seemed to have the right ideas, and I thought we could achieve a lot together. After the failure of Harry Viljoen's era, it seemed a more propitious time for Springbok rugby when Straeuli took over.

But gradually, as time passed, he wanted more control. He wanted to control everything: the players, the coaching staff, the media … everyone. Adriaan Heijns may have contributed to that, but in fairness, I'd say Rudi is a little like that anyway. Perhaps he was too stubborn, too inflexible to be a long-term success in the job. You have to understand that everybody has a different way of doing things, and that's fair enough. Rudi was convinced the methods he relied on would work, and they were non-negotiable. After all, they had worked for him with Natal in the Currie Cup and at Super 12 level with the Sharks. So why wouldn't they for South Africa?

The answer is, success within a rugby team is a combination of a number of things. No.1, talent; No. 2, finding a coach who can get the players to play for him, to produce their best each time they go out; and No. 3, good team spirit. Some of these factors you can influence by what you do, but sometimes they just happen, they just come together.

For example, team spirit is only something you talk about when you lose. You never hear players talking about it when things are going well. The fact is, if you are a winning team, the team spirit is always good. If you are losing, it doesn't mean that the team spirit is bad, but, equally, it is not something that can be forced. It grows over a period of time. I am not sure Rudi understood that, because sometimes he tried to do things that forced team spirit, like compulsory drinks at sessions clearly intent on encouraging team bonding. But it doesn't work in those circumstances. It cannot be imposed.

Basically, Rudi had one way of doing things, and anyone who didn't agree with it was not a 'team man'. Rudi also didn't know when to take his foot off the pedal. It was a world away from the Mallett era. Ultimately, Rudi was probably too conservative, too traditional. We had gone on eight years from the 1995 World Cup win. And how many changes had occurred in eight years of modern, professional rugby?

In the end, it wasn't any one thing that convinced me that Rudi Straeuli was losing it, but the evidence began to mount up.

Before the 2003 Tri-Nations match in Pretoria against New Zealand, Rudi insisted the reserves had to participate in a trial match during the week leading up to the test. We had a huge contact session on the Wednesday, just seventy-two hours before taking on the All Blacks, and then the trial match. The reserves, even the injured players, had to get out there. It was madness. Afterwards, there were so many injuries, bumps and bruises that we didn't even know what the bench would be for the test. This possibly contributed to the 16-52 hammering we were given by New Zealand. It was a totally unnecessary session so close to the test.

Then, when we flew up to Pretoria for the game, we again drove past the usual hotel we stayed at in Johannesburg, the Intercontinental Palazzo at Montecasino. Instead, we headed right out of town and stayed at a hotel in the bush between Johannesburg and Pretoria. Rudi didn't want us distracted by the press and the agents who usually hang around the hotel foyers.

Although the new place was great if you wanted a weekend in the country, it caused all kinds of logistical trouble for the players. They had arranged for match tickets to be left at the Palazzo, where we thought we would be staying. Suddenly, we had to start making calls to that hotel and to family and friends, telling them we wouldn't be there, and where they could collect the tickets. This was on the Friday before the game. You don't want those distractions so close to an important test match, and maybe all that nonsense partly explains the shocking result. Of course, such a defeat was unacceptable, but I'd say those distractions definitely contributed to the outcome.

Players like routine before a big game, and when it is disrupted, they can get tense. Players already are very nervous before a game, and because of that, you don't need anything to upset them. What calms the nerves is routine, but, without it, as happened in this case, your mental preparation is disturbed. Brent Russell, for example, left his gum guard at the hotel, and had a shocker of a game.

Personally, I wasn't like that. They could have put me anywhere the night before. I just wanted to go and play. But I knew a lot of the other guys were different.

Rudi took the New Zealand defeat very hard, and so did the players, who were pretty miserable. Not long after, we had to go to Australia, and when we arrived in Brisbane, there were plenty of problems to sort out. There were team meetings with the players, and I had to find out what was bothering them. But they often wouldn't say what they were unhappy about, perhaps because it might seem as if they were ungrateful about the opportunity to play for South Africa. The view is always that you should just shut up and do your job. But that attitude doesn't help solve anything.

I tried to deal with those situations as well as I could, but to complicate matters further, Rudi and I differed on the way to handle such problems. I think if the players want you to go and tuck them in at night, then just do it as long as it makes them happy. Because in the end, it is more important to win a test match than to complain that one or two players need to be spoon-fed. In that squad, probably five or six of them would have wanted that, which is, quite frankly, quite a lot. But remember, we were a very young group of players.

It is hard to criticise Rudolf, because he is a goodhearted person, and he is still my friend. I'm sorry if what I have to say hurts him, but I have to be honest. He made too many mistakes, and we paid the price for it.

Could we have won the 2003 World Cup under someone else as coach? I don't think so; I don't think we had the players. And that wasn't Rudi's fault.

I partly blame the selection panel, those at SA Rugby, for choosing Rudi in the first place. I don't think he had enough coaching experience at the time to be successful in the top job. He was thrown in at the deep end. He should have coached a provincial side for a few more years and gained more experience in handling players. Had they chosen someone else at the time and given Rudi the job a few years later, it might well have worked out more successfully.

But Straeuli took over as Springbok coach when he wasn't yet up to the task. That wasn't his fault. It might be disappointing for him to hear that, but I say it as someone who likes him and enjoyed him as a person. He just wasn't the right man to coach South Africa at that time, and subsequent events proved me right.

11
Through the Looking Glass

No one was more excited or thrilled than me when the Springboks won the 2004 Tri-Nations. It had been a long time coming. We had not been able to call ourselves champions of the southern hemisphere since 1998, and in each of those intervening five seasons, we had ended at the bottom of the log.

Mind you, even the 2004 Springboks could not compare with the team of 1998. Then, they won all four matches, finishing with 17 points. Australia, who were runners-up, finished on 10 points. In 2004, like the other two countries, we won two and lost two, but took the title by 11 points to 10 from Australia, because we picked up an extra bonus point.

But 2004 was a special year nevertheless. The Springboks won the IRB's Team of the Year, Schalk Burger won Player of the Year and Jake White won Coach of the Year. Springbok rugby was once again able to hold its head high.

This success, however, may not necessarily herald the start of a long, successful run as the top dogs in the southern hemisphere. New Zealand – remarkably enough without a World Cup triumph since way back in 1987 – took the chance to remind the world that they are gearing up for a major assault on the 2007 trophy by thrashing the British & Irish Lions in June/July 2005. Then they confirmed the growing pool of talent at their disposal by winning the Tri-Nations in September 2005, beating Australia by 10 points in the last match of the tournament. However, don't write off the Australians. I was very impressed by how well they competed with what was basically a B team. They managed to score four tries against the All Blacks, which just goes to show how good their running lines are. But, on the day, I think New Zealand deserved to win.

Teams, like results, come and go. England were hopeless for years, yet suddenly, around 2000, they began to build a formidable side and duly won the 2003 World Cup. We did the same in 1995 at the World Cup. And we may be gearing up for the 2007 World Cup in much the same way. With two more years to go, things are looking very positive for the Springboks.

There are a few elements a successful side must have behind them: the organisation, the business acumen, the vision and the ability to put all those elements into place for the benefit of those playing the game. An excellent back-up team is required to support the on-field team if proper success is not only to be achieved, but sustained. After all, it's not much use being successful one year and being roundly beaten the next. The Springboks under Jake White are slowly but surely getting there. In the 2005 Tri-Nations competition, they won as many games as New Zealand, and one more than they won the year before.

The true definition of a top-quality sports team is sustained success. Under the present system and with the personnel currently involved off the field, I fear that may well be beyond our capabilities. Yet I sincerely hope I am proved wrong. I'd love to see the Boks go to the next World Cup and win it. That would be fantastic for this country. But I wonder …

I wonder whether we have the right people behind the scenes running the game when so many spats become public concerning South African rugby, when so much dirty linen is regularly aired in public. It is unseemly, and yet hardly a week seems to go by without one administrator verbally attacking another, or administrators either resigning or being accused of mismanagement, thus disrupting the smooth running of the game.

If you are a supporter like me, on the outside looking in, you are entitled to have your say and make your views known. We live in a democracy now, and why shouldn't we stand up and say what we believe?

But those running SA Rugby are not in that position. They

need to give an impression of harmony, of people working together towards a common goal: the upliftment of South African rugby. But plainly, that has not been the case in recent times.

In April 2005, the president of SARU,* Brian van Rooyen, and François Pienaar, CEO of the RWC Bid Company, travelled overseas to try to bolster South Africa's chances of staging the 2011 World Cup. They toured the British Isles and Ireland, pressing the flesh and building up support. But what was happening back home in the meantime?

In effect, a palace coup was being mounted against Van Rooyen's presidency. Those who presumably said at one point that they supported him were now agitating against him behind his back, jockeying for position should they succeed in toppling the president. This was more in accordance with a South American banana republic back in the 1970s when a leader couldn't leave his country for fear of being overthrown in his absence. This is not how you run a country, or a sports governing body, for that matter.

Such a situation hardly casts South African rugby in a positive light. What would people around the world have thought when the news broke of what had been going on while the president was overseas? Any governing body loses kudos in those circumstances, and South African rugby would have suffered.

But that is just one example of what appears to be chaotic management of the game by those at the top. Van Rooyen came into office talking of the need to sort out budgets and clear huge deficits, while apparently supporting the players and Springbok rugby. He then tried to put an end to the playing contracts that SA Rugby had in place, and only backed down when it appeared that the players themselves might go to court over the issue. Van Rooyen was proposing huge match fees for each game played, but no monthly retainer. This was obviously unacceptable. For

* The name change from SARFU to SARU (South African Rugby Union) had occurred in November 2004.

example, how can a rugby player buy a house if he doesn't know how much he earns from one month to the next?

Furthermore, should a player be seriously injured while representing South Africa, he would not be entitled to any money from SA Rugby. This is appalling. You cannot treat professional sportsmen in so cavalier a manner in the modern world.

While all these negotiations were going on, Van Rooyen decided to publish the Springbok salaries on the front page of a local newspaper. A shrewd move, as it got the public behind him. One can only imagine what the average rugby supporter, who earns a modest monthly income and spends about R300 of that on an M-Net subscription, must have made of the fact that two Springbok players, including me, earned in excess of a million rand in 2003. And that they had the nerve to demand not only match fees, but also a retainer!

Van Rooyen was in breach of contract when he disclosed the players' salaries. The contracts contain a confidentiality clause barring the disclosure of any information on individuals' remuneration. Had I had a contract at the time, I would have taken Van Rooyen to court.

There was no question that SA Rugby had the money to fund the player contracts. No wonder the players' representatives refused to accept such a proposal, and today the players have their contracts.

I think it's fair to say that the South African public has been forced to sit and watch these regular farcical shows and verbal altercations among those at the top of the South African game for far too long. In time that should have been devoted to strengthening the game in our country, to ensuring we have the proper and correct playing structure in terms of competitions and schedules, far too many elected officials have been wasting time arguing and scrapping with each other, and, at best, coming up with ridiculous schemes and ideas that have no value whatsoever. It has been a depressing situation, and I can honestly say I don't think we have seen the end of it. I won't mind betting that the petty squabbling will go on indefinitely, reappearing from time to time.

If that is the case, all the promise that exists in South African rugby in terms of the many excellent players who continue to emerge will again be largely wasted. And, let's face it, we South Africans are most adept at wasting talent. We're probably the best in the world at allowing high-class players to slip through our fingers.

Take a look at a shortlist of some of the players who have left South African rugby in recent years and gone on to make their mark for another rugby nation. Australia recruited the services of the wing Clyde Rathbone and lock Daniel Vickermann; England snapped up Mike Catt and Matt Stevens. But that tells only half the story. Look at the talented players who left this country when they still had so much to offer South African rugby: Selborne Boome, Jake Boer, Robbie Fleck, Marius Hurter, André Vos, Bob Skinstad, Percy Montgomery, Japie Mulder, Cobus Visagie, Brendan Venter, Naka Drotske, Gary Teichmann, Stefan Terblanche, Jaco van der Westhuyzen, Gary Pagel, Christo Bezuidenhout, Thinus Delport, Robbie Kempson and many, many others.

Granted, several of them left only when they had ended their international careers. One cannot blame players who have been offered very lucrative deals, perhaps for two to three years with a northern hemisphere club, for wanting to take up those offers. The attraction of the pound or euro at the current exchange rate will continue to entice players overseas when they believe their international career is over. I was one of them.

But I wonder just how much effort was made to persuade those players to remain in South Africa. Were they told that they were still wanted and that it would be very unfortunate, a huge loss, if they went? Somehow, I doubt it. I know it certainly didn't happen in my case.

It is not just Springbok rugby that loses out when a former international finishes playing. If that player goes abroad, his value in playing the last two or three seasons at home in a provincial side is also lost. And that is where his worth would be at its greatest. Young players trying to make their way in the game need senior players alongside them in order to gain from their experience. As a youngster, you cannot learn the game as thoroughly if you are in a side without experienced players. The immense amount of knowledge they are able to pass on is of huge value. But if that player is not offered a financial incentive at least comparable with what he may be earning abroad, then of course he will go.

But imagine a scenario in which SARU declared that they no longer wanted to see their top former internationals going abroad. They would therefore create a financial pot, a fund from which they could draw monies to help enhance a senior player's wages if he remained at home in South Africa to help the next generation come through. Either that, or create a fund for the purposes of awarding financial bonuses after a specific time in the role. Either way, the game in South Africa would benefit hugely from seeing so many more of those guys staying put.

You will never stop every single player from going overseas; that would be impossible. But I think if it was made worthwhile for players to stay in South Africa, a lot more might reject the thought of a long, hard English winter and decide to stay at home. South African rugby would be the winner, of that I am certain.

Is it possible? A sponsoring company may want to look closely at such a proposal. Positive assistance for the game in this country will most certainly garner favourable publicity, which would be mutually beneficial to both parties.

I am not saying this is necessarily the answer to the problem. Perhaps someone can come up with a better plan. But I believe we should start looking at the possibilities and turn them into realities for the future benefit of South African rugby.

Very few players who return after an overseas stint ever receive a phone call from SARU, asking for their input. No one says, 'Look, it would be great if you could get involved.' No one says that they'd like to see whether the player's experience could be used in some way to help future Springboks. I haven't asked them, but I doubt very much whether the likes of Mark Andrews, Japie Mulder or Gary Pagel ever received such a call.

I suspect this is a widespread failure on the part of the game worldwide. I remember reading about Gareth Edwards, who said that he and his old mates from those great Welsh glory days were never asked to help Welsh rugby when it was at rock bottom in the 1980s and 1990s. Administrators around the world don't seem to want others to get involved. Somehow, they seem threatened by such assistance, and I find that incomprehensible.

If Welsh rugby could not find a single role for someone as esteemed as Gareth Edwards, one of the greatest players the game has ever known, then I probably shouldn't be surprised that our administrators don't seem to want to call on the talent of so many former players either. But I do believe our game would be strengthened if they were asked to help.

One thing we all have in common is our love for the game in this country. We want to see future generations make the Springboks the top rugby team in the world. I would have thought that any possible means to create that situation would have been explored. But if this is to happen, our administrators are going to have to become a lot more adept at running a rugby union than has been the case so far.

They would have to start bringing people together instead of dividing them with their frequent squabbles and bouts of infighting. They will have to demonstrate true leadership, and that requires vision, an ability to utilise the skills of all those available to the organisation, and making the most of the resources available. It has to mean that rugby union in this country becomes, if you like, a broad church, a body that welcomes everyone who shares its aspirations and motives into its midst.

But until that starts to happen, I suspect I am not alone in doubting the ability of South African rugby to really fulfil its obvious potential.

Another area in which I see great room for improvement is in the selection of a national coach. Frankly, South Africa's method of appointing a coach is a hit-and-miss affair.

Personally, I believe the selectors should have brought Nick Mallett back for the good of South African rugby, rather than appointing Rudolf Straeuli when they did. But I suppose that was never on the agenda. Nor was it ever likely they would appoint an overseas coach, someone like John Mitchell of New Zealand or England's Clive Woodward. It was always going to be another South African. Would it work if New Zealand appointed a South African or an Englishman to coach them? I don't know. Can you see the All Blacks ever doing that? Of course not.

But that isn't to say we should summarily dismiss such an idea. For example, what might an audacious offer to Clive Woodward, after he had led England to the 2003 World Cup, have produced? I suspect a great deal of interest on Clive's part.

I am by no means offering a blueprint on how to run the game in this country. I just want to draw attention to the kind of possibilities that exist these days, and offer a few ideas as to how national unions can get their decisions right and expand their business.

As I've said before in this book, of those candidates inside South Africa, I still think Nick Mallett is potentially the best Springbok coach – provided, of course, he is still interested in the job. Mallett has a proven record both with the Boks and overseas, and at forty-eight he is still young enough for the job. If South African rugby does not utilise his talents once again before it is too late, it will be a terrible waste.

Although Mallett is back in South Africa as Director of Rugby with Western Province, it's a bit like taking Jean de Villiers or Schalk Burger out of the current Springbok side and making them team manager. Is that where you are going to see their skills best utilised? Mallett is much the same. I know he will influence playing policy in his new position and be as hands-on as possible. But Nick's greatest talent lies in coaching teams. He commands huge respect from his players and, best of all, he shares the passion he has for rugby with his players, managing to impart that passion to his team so that it shows in their game.

But coaching, at least for now, seems safe in the hands of Jake White. Jake's appointment had also had its share of farcical elements, and once again, I thought disaster was looming. Jake had not even been on the original shortlist of candidates! Only when three of the four candidates withdrew was Jake's name added to the list.

I have to hand it to Jake – he has done a fantastic job in uplifting the Springbok game, and he thoroughly deserved to be IRB Coach of the Year in 2004. I hope his successes continue well into 2007 and beyond. Only one thing concerns me at this stage: the Springboks' reliance on the opposition making mistakes, on which they then capitalise. We are not creating tries from constructive play. I believe Jake will sort this shortcoming out as the confidence within the team grows.

There are other problems in South African rugby that also need looking at. The structures that have been set up are not conducive to growing the game in this country. There are fourteen rugby unions, of which five are very big and have turnovers of close to R100 million a year. The other nine are small, and all struggle financially. The representatives of the fourteen unions vote in the president of SARU. The problem is, their votes all count the same.

During 2002, SA Rugby appointed the company Accenture to research the running of SA Rugby and make recommendations. The most pertinent recommendation Accenture made was for the Currie Cup to revert back to a strength-versus-strength structure in two sections. That is to say, the five big unions and one other would play each other home and away, with promotion–relegation in place. This was agreed, and the new structure was supposed to have been implemented in 2003. One problem, however! Van Rooyen had managed to rally all the small unions behind him before the election of the new president. Voting for him would mean an opportunity to play in the Currie Cup and a R2-million grant from SARFU, saving them from certain bankruptcy.

Needless to say, Van Rooyen was voted in, and the Currie Cup is back to square one. In 2005, nobody really knows what is going to happen to the Currie Cup competition. SARU recommended that ten Springbok players be rested after the 2005 Tri-Nations for the end-of-year tour to Wales and France. I think it is a great idea, but how can one really expect a union like Natal to rest a player whom they are paying R1 million a year? Why are all the top Boks not contracted by SARU instead?

These and many other issues will have to be sorted out in the foreseeable future if South African rugby is to reach its true potential, and the Springboks reign as world champions once more. Let's hope that sanity will prevail, and the good of South African rugby is placed before personal interest.

12
The Last Hurrah

It had always been my intention to go abroad. I always had very clear ideas as to what I wanted to achieve in rugby, and playing abroad for two years and then retiring at the age of thirty was very clearly mapped out in my mind.

When I sat down with my agent and discussed the possibilities, France was my first choice. I really wanted to go to Biarritz. I'd heard so much about this charming town in south-west France, nestled between the Atlantic coast and the Pyrenees. The border with Spain was just a stone's throw away. The setting appealed to me, and I'd heard from several sources that there was a fine rugby club with strong traditions in the town. I wasn't concerned about the language difficulty; I felt I could learn a new language, and really fancied the challenge, both on and off the field.

There was just one problem. Biarritz, it turned out, didn't want me. They had Serge Betsen in their back row, who played a similar role to the one I would have offered. So that was a non-starter.

Today, knowing a lot more about French rugby, Stade Toulouse would be my first choice. They are the Manchester United of European rugby, a club with a fabulous history and pedigree, great facilities and a budget to match.

But a call came through to Cape Town in the first few months of 2004 that changed all my plans. Alan Solomons, the coach with whom I'd enjoyed working so much at Western Province, had left three seasons earlier to join the Irish provincial side Ulster, based in Belfast. Alan and I had had a fantastic working relationship in Cape Town, and when he left to go overseas, he and I both said that we'd very much like to work together again at some point in the future.

So there was always that feeling that we might touch base again at some stage. But I didn't expect what happened next. As far as I was aware, Solly was staying with Ulster, for whom he was doing a fine job. But then he phoned me to say he'd just signed a two-year contract with the English Premiership club Northampton Saints, and might I be interested in joining him there.

Solly said he was also signing other South African players, such as Robbie Kempson and Selborne Boome. I thought about it briefly, and felt it would be great to link up with Solly again. The fact that I would sign with a big English Premiership club (they had been European champions in 2000) only added to the attraction.

Gary Pagel, the Springbok prop in our 1995 World Cup–winning side, had also played for Northampton, and I spoke to him about the club. He told me he'd loved every minute of his time there, and that it was a really nice club in a true rugby town. He assured me that I would enjoy it. Then I called Selborne Boome, who had already visited the club, and he reported a very organised, professional outfit, saying he had no doubts about his move. Considering such recommendations, as well as the fact that Solly was going to be there, I signed without even going to see the club or the town. I put my signature to a two-year deal and was sure I'd made the right choice.

Western Province were very understanding when I told them about my decision. They knew I was coming to the end of my career and that I had always expressed an interest in playing overseas in my final few years. They said they would release me after the Springboks returned from the Tri-Nations campaign around the end of August 2004.

My last match for Western Province turned out to be a very emotional occasion for me. It was against Griquas at Newlands, a ground I had come to love, together with all the great fans who had supported me through the years. Western Province were very kind – they even invited all the surgeons who had operated on me during my career to attend the farewell function as guests! I felt very emotional.

I'd been saying to the guys throughout the Currie Cup campaign that I would like to drop a goal before I ended my Western Province career. The great Frik du Preez, one of South African rugby's best-ever forwards, had famously dropped a goal, scored a try and kicked a conversion in a test match. I knew I had some way to go to match that!

But when we led Griquas something like 40-10 in the second half, I decided the moment had come. I can't pretend it matched Jannie de Beer's effort of five dropkicks in the 1999 World Cup match against England in Paris; in fact, this one was from close to the posts. But I'll tell you this, the surge of pleasure and satisfaction when the ball sailed between those posts was immense! And to round it all off nicely, I also scored a try and made a conversion attempt in the last minute. Unfortunately, I couldn't choose the position for that kick, and it was from way out near the touchline. Predictably, I missed it. Still, I couldn't have been happier with the way the match and the whole occasion had gone.

I had hugely enjoyed my years at Western Province. Sure, we'd had good times and bad times, successes and failures. We had tasted triumph, but also the bitter pill of defeat, when you come up just short. That Super 12 semi-final loss against Otago at Newlands was one of the biggest setbacks. If we'd won, we would have had the final at home.

But there were Currie Cup wins and some notable performances. I want to stress how deeply I appreciated the support I always received from the Western Province people. A player feels so much better about himself and what he is trying to do with the team if he knows he has the backing of the supporters. I have to admit that some of the scrapes I got into with Western Province were not always very clever. But I always felt that those who were true fans, who knew their rugby, were on my side, and I was very grateful for that.

One of my final acts for the Stormers was certainly not one of the cleverest in my career. In the 2004 Super 12, we won our first two overseas games of the competition, including beating the Auckland Blues on their own patch by the huge margin of 51-23, an eight-try hammering of epic proportions. The previous week, we'd beaten the Queensland Reds in Brisbane 21-20. No South African team had ever won its first two overseas Super 12 games away from home. That was something new and very promising as we looked ahead to the remainder of the season.

But then we played the Chiefs in Waikato, and they frustrated us by cleverly slowing our ball down. We had mostly beaten them in previous Super 12 matches and were confident of doing so again. But they smothered our game, making life very tough for us. Unfortunately, I reacted to it. I dived into a ruck head first, missed the guy who was hanging around illegally on our side, their centre Derek Maisey, but then stupidly stepped back and had another go at him. This time, I connected. He just walked away, but after the game the citing commissioner cited me. I knew at once what a disastrous act of indiscipline it would prove to be.

The outcome of that match and the banning I received afterwards were of the lowest points in my whole career. I was banned for eight weeks for the headbutt, and we went on to lose the match 14-29. In fact, we lost three of our last four matches, yet still qualified for the semi-finals. Unfortunately, I couldn't take part in it, and we had to cross twenty time zones in the course of just nine days to play against the Crusaders twice in a fortnight. It was asking the impossible of fifteen very brave men. The Stormers even led 13-12 at half-time, before a combination of jet lag and the Crusaders' power overwhelmed us in the last forty minutes.

I never wanted my Stormers Super 12 career to end on such a note, and I took some fearful stick from the South African media over the incident. Some of it was fair comment; others went completely over the top. One article was the worst I ever read about myself; it really hurt me, and my wife was very upset too.

But I guess if you hand these guys a stick with which to beat you, they'll grab it.

Often, when you remove a rugby player from the intensity and height of the action and ask him to analyse something he did, he is almost bewildered at his actions. Now, when I look back at that Super 12 incident and the events at Twickenham, I just think to myself: 'Was that really me?' I still ask myself how I could have done those things. I abhor violence. I have a young family and have no wish to seek confrontation of any kind.

I can only assume that people do such things under the ferocious pressures of the occasion. There are no 'normal' pressures in a rugby game, and therefore people do not always react rationally. Of course, I always regretted these incidents afterwards. But by then it is too late. The emotion of the moment takes over to such an extent that you find yourself committing an act that you would never otherwise imagine doing.

Certainly, I deeply regretted the Chiefs incident. I had played sixty-three Super 12 matches for the Stormers, and being banned was a lousy way to bow out. The ban not only cost me my place in a Super 12 semi-final, but also my position in a Barbarians team to play in the UK. They couldn't pick someone who was serving a lengthy ban in his own country, and I understood their decision. But even worse, I had let down my Stormers' teammates and our many supporters, all of whom had been with me all the way, encouraging and supporting me during every season. In one mad moment, I had wrecked it all, and it's something I still bitterly regret. The depressing end of my Super 12 career will stay with me for the rest of my life, and I don't exaggerate when I say that I still find it painful to remember.

In the end, I flew to the UK in early September, leaving Justine behind for the first month. But almost immediately I encountered my first problem. Before I left Cape Town, Solly had told me he wanted me to be his captain. But by the time I arrived in Northampton, I had missed the entire pre-season training programme, normally a key time for a new captain to settle in and get acquainted with his players. I discussed the implications with Solly, and said that I thought it would be very difficult for me to go straight in as captain. But he just said, 'If I thought you couldn't handle it, I wouldn't have offered.' So I accepted the challenge and assured him I wanted to make a real go of it.

I didn't find it easy adapting to life on or off the field. The weather was very different to a Cape Town autumn, when you still expect temperatures anywhere between 20 and 30°C. There was some sunshine, but it certainly wasn't warm. Also, I found simple things like opening a bank account incredibly complicated; it took me three weeks to complete that process. It was a very challenging and difficult time, but I stayed positive.

I had a little apartment very close to the club's Franklin's Gardens ground, and it was good to hear plenty of South African accents around the place. There were six South Africans in all: Alan Solomons, Selborne Boome, Robbie Kempson (who had followed Solly across from Ulster), Johan van Wyk, Wylie Human and me. Definitely too many, with hindsight.

I knew that if I was going to make a success of the captaincy, I couldn't show any favouritism towards my fellow South Africans. There were also three New Zealanders, a Scotsman and lots of English players there, several of whom I had tangled with during England–South Africa internationals.

There was another difficulty too. Early in 2004, the Northampton and England scrumhalf Matt Dawson had published his autobiography, *Nine Lives*, in which he described me as 'thug in chief' for my actions during the Twickenham game in 2002. Dawson wrote: 'Krige was caught on film, launching into my head with a flying butt. He also caught me in the face with a blatant forearm smash, which, after thudding against me, put his own teammate André Pretorius out of the game. Krige was also seen punching Jason and Jonny and attempting to do the same to Lawrence Dallaglio. Before he was finished, he stamped on Phil

Vickery and planted a shoulder into Mike Tindall. It was inexcusable behaviour.'

Later in the book, he wrote: 'My nemesis, Corné Krige, has joined Northampton as club captain. I'm glad I've moved on [to London Wasps] as he's not the sort of person I'd want as my captain.'

Those words threatened to make life very difficult for me when I arrived at Northampton. Initially, there was some talk about Saints season-ticket-holders protesting my presence at the club, and particularly my appointment as captain. Some threatened to return their tickets. Doubtless, they had been heavily influenced by Dawson's words. One reporter wrote that, although Saints fans might be happy to embrace a loose trio consisting of 'Corné Krige, Freddy Krueger and Osama bin Laden if it guaranteed them winning the Premiership, the Powergen Cup and the Heineken Cup', I would have to work hard to shake my bad-boy image in England. I found it very funny.

As regards Matt Dawson, he seemed to be a man unwilling to accept an apology. Since that day at Twickenham, I have stated on more than one occasion, with total sincerity, that what I did was wrong, and that I bitterly regretted my actions. But Dawson doesn't seem able to accept my apology. I find that most unfortunate. Perhaps it reflects more on him than me, who made the mistakes. Sometimes you have to put your hand up and admit that you were wrong, and sometimes you have to be big enough to accept an apology. It isn't always easy, especially if you are a proud person. I knew I'd been in the wrong, and I said I was sorry. Perhaps Matt Dawson just wasn't big enough to accept it.

Matt Dawson's autobiography meant I had quite a difficult time of it when I was introduced to the press soon after my arrival at Northampton. I didn't want Solly to break the news of my captaincy as soon as I arrived. I felt it would have been better to announce it a few days later.

But on my first day at the club, the players had gathered for a team photo in the presence of the media, and Solly made the announcement. I had to take my seat in the front row, holding the ball, for the team photo. I felt most uncomfortable, and the whistling from the players as I made my way to the front bench didn't help. They said things like, 'Here's Cappie, here's the main man.' It was all light-hearted enough, but I felt pretty uncomfortable. Some of the players I hadn't even met.

And the Dawson matter kept popping up. The media always wanted to drag it up as a story. But the strange thing was, once I had spent some time at the club, I began to understand that everything was not always as it seemed. Initially, I thought a lot of people were upset that Dawson had gone, but later I realised he hadn't been as popular as some people perceived.

I made my mind up to be positive about the captaincy, as I generally am in life. I spent those first few weeks alone, reflecting hard on my life and what I had achieved. I used that time to think carefully on both the high and lows of my life, and it quickly dawned on me just how privileged I had been to have had a great career with Western Province, the Stormers and South Africa.

Eventually the talking stopped and the playing began. We won our first game at home, against Bath, but I have to admit, I was surprised at how physical and dirty it was. At one stage, Bath's England lock Danny Grewcock ran all over Selborne Boome as he lay on the ground, from his ankles right up to his head. I was furious about it, but knew I had to stay out of disciplinary matters. Imagine the headlines in the English media the next day if I'd got involved with Grewcock: 'Krige at it again' …

I expected to be picked on by touch judges and referees too, so I was very careful about what I did. And I succeeded, because I never received one red or yellow card during the entire season with Northampton.

In fact, there's a funny story about that. After my last game at Franklin's Gardens, a stranger came up to me and said simply,

'I've a cheque for you.' Apparently, he and a few of his pals had decided before the season began that they would put money into a general kitty for every game in which I was not awarded a yellow or red card. By the end of the season, without a single card to my name, the kitty had grown to £128, and he duly presented me with the cheque. I was astonished. A bit of fun and a nice gesture; thanks, guys.

When we beat Harlequins in our next match, we had taken 10 points from our first two matches and looked to be well on course for a highly successful season. Everyone was very positive and there was a fantastic atmosphere. There was even early talk about the club winning the Zurich Premiership title. The supporters had been apprehensive about all the changes, but once we started playing, they got right behind us.

But I was aware of potential problems all the time. I wondered how I would have felt if an English coach had been appointed at Western Province and brought in six players from England. And how would I have felt if I'd seen how he was trying to change our culture? I would like to think that, as a player, I would have been professional enough to support him. But that still didn't solve the problems I knew existed. With a South African coach, a maximum of two South African players would have been enough. In that respect, I have to say that Alan Solomons underestimated the local feelings at the club. It was too much of a culture shock to suddenly bring six South Africans into the Saints squad. However, I don't think Northampton have learnt their lesson, because by the time the 2005/06 English season kicked off, they'd recruited four New Zealanders.

And of course, the problems did come – thick and fast – after our great start. After winning our first two league matches, we suddenly lost eight games in a row. Many were very close matches: for example, we lost at home to London Wasps by a single point, not a bad result when you consider they went on to become Zurich Premiership champions for the third year running. And we had opportunities to win the game too, twice missing crucial penalty kicks.

But then we went to Leicester, and they ran up 30 points against us. In fact, it was the only game in the eight defeats where we were beaten hands down.

Alan Solomons and I found ourselves under increasing pressure. There was growing disquiet, and all the old doubts began to be voiced again. At one point, our physio Cliff Eaton approached me and said that the senior players were having a meeting without my knowledge. He said, 'I think you should address the issue and find out what is happening.' I agreed.

I was very shocked that the senior guys would conspire behind my back. So I went to Paul Grayson, who has been at Northampton for years and is one of their playing legends, and Tom Smith, our Scottish and former British Lions prop, and said that we ought to have another meeting that also involved me. The three of us sat down and discussed the matter. They said that things had to change, as they didn't agree with some of Alan Solomons' ways.

It has always been one of Solly's coaching traits that he relies on his players to discipline themselves within the system. He didn't enjoy enforcing discipline, although he would if it was absolutely necessary. But generally he treated players like adults, and expected them to behave as such.

I suggested having a meeting with Solly in which the player's views could be aired. I found it disturbing that they'd had their own meeting without approaching him in the first instance. Obviously matters were not as they should have been at the club. But during the players' meeting with Solly, they told him they wanted more responsibility for themselves, and he said he would take their views 'on board'.

Unfortunately, after we had lost the previous weekend, making it seven defeats on the trot, Keith Barwell, the owner of the club, had been in to see Solly. Rightly or wrongly, people assumed that Solly was on his way out, and the rumour spread.

My teammates often told me that I needed to shout and scream at them when things were not going right on the field. But I told them that wasn't my style; it wasn't me. So I had a word with Steve Thompson, who was vice-captain, and told him that if shouting or screaming were required during a match, he should do it.

The trouble was, although Thompson had won the World Cup with England a year earlier, he was still a very young, largely inexperienced player. He didn't really know what life was all about. Although he had experience of the game, he still had lots to learn in terms of understanding people.

I went to see Steve after Solly had handed me a newspaper article in which Lawrence Dallaglio had said that Thompson, not me, should captain the Saints. I asked Steve if he had a problem with me as captain, because, quite honestly, I wasn't that keen on the role anyway. I would have been just as happy playing in the team under someone else's leadership.

Steve's reply took me slightly aback. He said, 'That article is exactly what Englishmen are all about: kick a man when he is down.' So I took Steve at his word and got on with the job.

English Premiership rugby is very simple. You are basically required just to dominate in the forwards and put yourself in position to kick penalties or score tries. Knowing that, we should have won more games, but it didn't happen. And when we lost at home to Worcester, who had only been promoted to the Premiership that season, the writing was on the wall. Alan Solomons was fired.

I was very disappointed to see him go. Solly was a friend of mine, and I'd known him a long time. I knew that he was a good coach, as well as a good man. He didn't deserve to be treated in that way, and when a friend gets treated badly by his employers, you feel bad about it too. But everything he'd tried had back-fired on him.

I know that certain senior players had worked against Solly

to get him out. Solly had told Ben Cohen, the former England wing, that he should look for another club because he wasn't a team man. Solly wanted team players, and therefore would not sign Cohen the following year. Cohen said to me some time later, 'I realised then that it was either him or me, and I decided there and then that it was going to be him who would go.'

I believe Cohen rallied other senior players against Solomons, like Paul Grayson, Tom Smith and Steve Thompson. Some players became very negative when things started to go wrong. And it only takes one guy to start the rot in that kind of situation. However, certainly not everyone was against Solly; a lot of the guys liked him.

When Solly was fired, I resigned at once as captain. I felt I had no choice. Solly had appointed me, and now he was gone. I therefore had no foundation on which to remain as captain. Two long-standing Northampton players, Budge Pountney and Paul Grayson, took over as joint coaches, Pountney as full-time coach because his playing days were over. Keith Barwell expressed the hope that Northampton's future long-term coaches would be from within the club, which was a clear indication that he was backing Pountney and Grayson. Subsequent events confirmed this. In July 2005, Pountney was appointed Director of Rugby at the club, with Grayson as first-team coach.

The week Solly left was the most bizarre you could ever imagine at a rugby club. Everything was chaotic because of the events taking place. And we were staring up at almost every other club from the bottom of the Premiership table. How quickly all my hopes, my ambitions and my plans with Alan Solomons had turned to dust. I thought about quitting, and it would have been the easiest thing in the world to do. I think I knew by that time I wouldn't be staying for the second year of my contract: indeed, I was already almost certain in my mind that I would retire from the game when the English season ended in May. But it would have been so easy to walk out right then. It was cold, wet and miserable in England. I could have taken my wife and new baby daughter, Sophia Maria, back to the sunshine of Cape Town, to all we knew and loved. But I didn't want to walk away in failure. I knew there was a big job to do that season, trying to keep Northampton in the Premiership, and I never wanted to be called a quitter. So I resolved to stay, and knuckled down to see the season through.

A lot of my teammates came to see me, saying they didn't think I should have stepped down as captain. I thanked them for their support, and I really appreciated their backing. But my decision to quit was the right one.

And given what happened subsequently, I was glad I'd resigned without being pushed. Because when Pountney and Grayson had a vote among the squad to see whom the players wanted as captain, Steve Thompson and I got exactly the same number of votes. I stood up and said that I thought Steve should be made captain, as I felt I'd be able to play better without that burden. They agreed with me, but asked me to stand in as captain when Steve went away to do duty with England.

The arrangement seemed perfectly normal and acceptable at the time. But months later, Budge Pountney told me that I had in fact got 95 per cent of the players' votes. I found their earlier announcement bizarre, to say the least. I believe their motivation was to rally the players behind Thompson.

Anyway, I don't think there is any doubt that I did play much better once I was free from the captaincy. I could concentrate fully on my own game and how I wanted to play, instead of worrying about the importance of the game and its outcome to the club. I no longer had to worry about how certain players might handle the pressure, or how various individuals would react to motivational talks before a game. All of the factors that a captain has to consider were no longer my responsibility.

We played Leicester at home and beat them, and although it was on an international weekend and both teams were without their England players, it was a fine victory. It lifted spirits considerably. I enjoyed it tremendously, as it was also the last game Martin Johnson and Neil Back would play for Leicester.

I also began to get to know my teammates better, and enjoyed their company. There was a growing sense of 'we're all in this together', and there were some fine players and outstanding people in the squad, such as New Zealanders Andrew Blowers, Bruce Reihana and Sharky Robinson, with whom I became good friends. The team began to think and act positively, even though our league position remained perilous and would do so right up to the last day of the season.

In the end, we eked out a few more victories, including some crucial ones over our fellow strugglers in the relegation zone. But everything still came down to the final match of the season, on Saturday 30 April. We had to travel to Worcester, one of our rivals for the relegation, while several other matches were equally crucial to the outcome.

It was a very tense afternoon, with everyone's nerves as taut as piano wire. Teams literally climbed four or five places up the table, or moved the same number of places down during the course of a game as they scored and other sides conceded tries. In the end, it was the London club NEC Harlequins who were relegated, after losing at home to Sale Sharks. Northampton lost 19-21 at Worcester, and but for the 22-23 Harlequins defeat, would have gone down.

I encountered a rather unpleasant facet of English rugby at Northampton, namely the way certain players from other clubs tried to provoke me. Naturally, I was convinced this was a spill-over from events at Twickenham two years earlier. Some of the players who went out of their way to needle me were well respected and held in high esteem in English rugby. Yet that didn't stop them from slyly punching me off the ball and trying to provoke a reaction from me – I suppose in the way I had done at Twickenham. But I am proud to say they never succeeded. I kept my composure and maintained discipline at all times. Part of the reason was, I half expected it and knew what might be coming.

When we played Leeds at Franklin's Gardens, one of their players threw five giant punches at my head during the game. It happened in full view of the referee, and all he did was award a penalty to us (which we then missed). I said to him, 'If that had been me, you'd have given me a red card.' He said nothing, because he knew he was in the wrong. I took my fair share of whacks, punches and kicks off the ball, but I'm mighty glad I never reacted to any of them.

During the last few months at the club, I began to notice that my body was struggling to deal with the physicality of the matches. And, unlike earlier in my career when I seemed to shake off bumps and bruises within a day or two, it was now taking three or four days to recover. Then I'd be close to the next match and another pounding. It became obvious that my body was trying to tell me something.

I knew by the end of the season that I would struggle to get through another pre-season with any club, let alone Northampton. I knew what the boys would face, as Budge Pountney loves fitness, and it was pretty clear they were going to get hammered. Somehow, I just couldn't see myself in that environment any more. I was thirty, I'd used and abused my body for long enough on the rugby grounds of the world, and I felt certain it was time to call it a day.

So I walked into the club one day, and told them I wanted to be released … to retire. In truth, they didn't try very hard to persuade me to stay an extra year. I think both parties understood that it was better for things to work out this way. I suppose I could have stayed at the club, gone through the motions, picked up a very handsome salary at the end of each month and just survived another twelve months. But for what? For the good of Northampton? For my own material well-being? No. I knew straightaway that if that was the case, then there was only one decision to make: quit. I have never conned a club in my life, and wasn't about to start now. Moreover, I didn't want people whispering among themselves that I wasn't the player I'd once been, that I'd lost my pace, my edge, my desire. I'd have hated to be in that situation, no matter how much I was being paid.

The honest course of action was therefore to announce my retirement and walk away. Which is what I did. I played a couple of end-of-season matches in the northern hemisphere, one with the Barbarians against England at Twickenham, and the other, the Martin Johnson testimonial game against a Jonah Lomu side, also at Twickenham. That took me up to June 2005, which is where it all ended for me.

One evening, I caught a cab to Heathrow, checked in for my flight to Cape Town and settled down in the seat for the journey home. As the aircraft climbed into the sky, I glanced out of the window to see a very famous rugby ground just underneath us: Twickenham. I think that was when the realisation hit me that I would never play on that ground, or any like it, ever again.

But even at that moment, and ever since, I have had no regrets about my decision. I am certain I made the right choice. The question of when to retire is probably the biggest a player will confront in his whole career, and it is essential to get the timing right. I believe I achieved that.

I am now immersing myself in business opportunities in Cape Town, and I'm sure that if I put as much work and dedication into that arena as I did into my rugby, I have every chance of being successful.

I do hope that business is different from rugby in that I will be afforded more time and opportunity to be successful than coaches in rugby football are given. When I look back and think about what happened to Alan Solomons at Northampton, I feel a mixture of bewilderment, frustration and pain for him. Solly had inherited a squad; the only new players he'd brought in were South Africans. Any coach needs time to be successful, and if

Northampton had been patient and stuck with Alan Solomons, I am certain they would have done better in the second half of the season. The following year could well have been the one in which he took the club to glory.

But that is the life of a coach. You live or die by your results. That's why you won't find me involved in top-level coaching. The job is far too precarious for my liking. You are dependent on others for your success, which is a strange situation to be in. If some of the Northampton players are honest, they will admit that they never sweated blood and guts to help Alan Solomons. There were many games that we lost by just a few points that could well have turned out differently if everyone had given more for the cause. Remember, the margins between winning and losing are often very small, and things could easily have turned out very differently.

But, for whatever reason, some players did not give their all, and I know this because, once Solly had left, I saw a difference in a few players' commitment. They suddenly started taking everything far more seriously. I know who they are, and they certainly know who they are, but I don't intend to name and shame them. They must live with their conscience, just like the rest of us.

At the end of the day, Northampton Rugby Club went back to traditional ways, sticking with people they knew, and who knew the club and its culture inside out. Yet I believe it is the influence of foreign coaches and players – South Africans, Australians, Frenchmen, Samoans, Kiwis, Welshmen, Scots and Irishmen, to mention a few – who have made the English Premiership the success it is. They have all had an input, bringing their own ideas and style to the proceedings. It has created a superb competition, and I don't know whether Northampton will find a successful formula simply by turning to the tried and trusted. Such a policy may come back to haunt them in the future – but that is their problem.

I like and respect Budge Pountney as a person. But I'll say this: he has to be very careful of the same people and players who turned on Alan Solomons. Who is to say that, after successfully getting rid of one man in charge, they won't manage it a second time if they don't like the way Pountney decides to do things? I admit that I lost my respect for some of the players because of their behaviour towards Solly.

But Northampton have been very clever in signing Carlos Spencer from New Zealand, who I believe will prove to be an outstanding signing, one of the best in the English Premiership. Carlos is a fantastic, very creative player. For New Zealand to allow him to leave says a lot about the strength in depth they have in their rugby right now.

As the giant aircraft circled high over London that Monday evening in June, I reflected long and hard on the ending of my rugby years and the new life I was about to enter. In my view, the money you earn from professional rugby is the easiest you will ever earn in your entire life. That's because you are playing a sport you love, and being paid to keep supremely fit and healthy. Unless you win the lottery, I don't see any better way of picking up significant sums of money.

Rugby has given me much else to be grateful for. It changed my life forever and afforded me fantastic opportunities. In so many ways, rugby gave me a head start in life. I will always be grateful that I could serve the game for the time given me.

Index

Do you have any comments, suggestions or feedback about this book or any other Zebra Press titles? Contact us at **talkback@zebrapress.co.za**